This book is for (Here Comes the Son-in-Law) Rich:
Love Is All You Need.

Published in 2020 by Welbeck

An Imprint of Welbeck Non-Fiction Limited, part of Welbeck
Publishing Group
20 Mortimer Street
London W1T 3JW

First published by Carlton Books Ltd in 2019

ISBN 978-1-78739-313-4

Editorial Director: Roland Hall
Art Editor: Russell Knowles
Picture Research: Steve Behan
Design: James Pople
Production: Rachel Burgess

A CIP catalogue for this book is available from the British Library

Printed in Dubai

10 9 8 7 6 5 4

THE BEATLES

ALBUM BY ALBUM

THE BAND AND THEIR MUSIC BY INSIDERS, EXPERTS AND EYEWITNESSES

Contributors

The Analogues' Diederik Nomden & Bart Van Poppel
The Bootleg Beatles • Tony Bramwell • Ray Connolly
Barbara Dickson • Tristan Fry • Per Gessle • Graham Gouldman
Steve Harley • Stephen James • Gered Mankowitz • Glen Matlock
Giles Martin • Chas Newby • Sir Tim Rice • David Roberts
Tom Robinson • Paul Sexton • Chris Thomas • Ken Townsend MBE
Johnnie Walker MBE • Kenneth Womack

General Editor and Contributor
BRIAN SOUTHALL

WELBECK

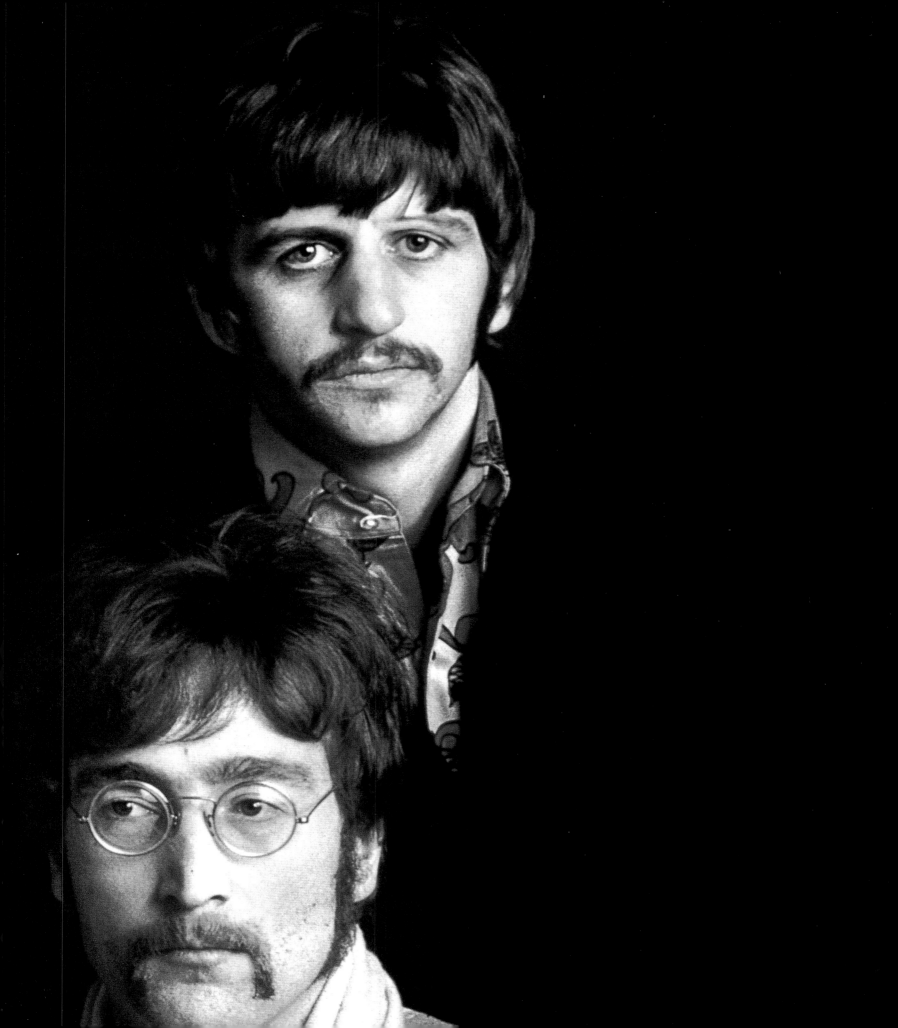

Contents

30

50

66

82

98

114

"Between 1963 and 1970 John Lennon, Paul McCartney, George Harrison and Ringo Starr dominated the airwaves and the charts with their music. For those of us who were around back then it was a magical, unforgettable time in our lives. From *Please Please Me* to *Let It Be* they set records and standards that arguably will never be broken or bettered."

Brian Southall

Contributors

Tony Bramwell grew up in Liverpool, went to school with George Harrison and worked for Brian Epstein at NEMS and for the Beatles in their Apple company. His autobiography *Magical Mystery Tours: My Life with the Beatles* was published in 2005.

Tristan Fry is a drummer and percussionist. He joined the London Philharmonic Orchestra aged 17 and played on sessions for the Beatles, Elton John and Olivia Newton-John before joining the hit-making jazz-rock fusion band Sky.

Ray Connolly is an award-winning journalist, screenwriter and novelist who met and interviewed the Beatles during the 1960s. He wrote the films *That'll Be The Day* and *Stardust*, starring David Essex, and the biography *Being John Lennon*, which came out in 2018.

Per Gessle was one half of the Swedish duo Roxette alongside Marie Fredriksson. They sold over 40 million records worldwide, including four US number ones, before embarking on solo careers and occasionally reuniting as Roxette.

Barbara Dickson was born in Scotland and appeared in the musicals *John, Paul, George, Ringo and Bert* and *Blood Brothers*. She has more than a dozen UK chart albums to her credit and six hit singles including the number one 'I Know Him So Well', with Elaine Paige.

Graham Gouldman wrote hits for Herman's Hermits, the Hollies and the Yardbirds before joining Eric Stewart, Lol Crème and Kevin Godley in 10cc in 1972. Included in their 13 UK hit singles are the #1 hits 'Rubber Bullets', 'I'm Not In Love' and 'Dreadlock Holiday'.

Opposite: 'I Want To Hold Your Hand' is a hit and the Beatles pose for a photo session in their dressing room.

Steve Harley is an ex-journalist who formed Cockney Rebel in 1974. Among his ten UK hits is the number one 'Make Me Smile (Come Up And See Me)' and the top ten records 'The Phantom Of The Opera' (with Sarah Brightman) and a cover version of the Beatles' 'Here Comes the Sun'.

Stephen James is the son of Dick James, the co-founder and director of the Beatles' music publishing company Northern Songs and Dick James Music. He worked with his father at both companies from 1963 and was instrumental in signing songwriters Elton John and Bernie Taupin.

Below: The Beatles on stage at White Sox Park – home to the Chicago White Sox baseball team – where they played two shows in August 1965.

Gered Mankowitz is an award-winning rock photographer who began working with the Rolling Stones in 1965 and went on to photograph Jimi Hendrix, Led Zeppelin, the Eurythmics, Kate Bush, Oasis and both Paul McCartney and George Harrison.

Glen Matlock joined the Swankers in 1973, two years before they became the Sex Pistols. He was in the band when they were sacked by EMI but left in 1977 and formed the Rich Kids. He has since played with the Damned and the Faces and on various Pistols reunions.

Giles Martin is the producer son of Sir George Martin. He has produced Elvis Costello and Kate Bush and worked with this father on the Beatles-inspired Cirque de Soleil production *Love*. He also oversaw the 50th anniversary deluxe reissues of *Sgt. Pepper's Lonely Hearts Club Band* and *The Beatles* ("The White Album").

Chas Newby is a member of the Liverpool band the Quarrymen, which was originally formed by John Lennon in 1957. He played four shows as a stand-in bass player with the Beatles in December 1960 and re-joined the Quarrymen in 2016.

Diederik Nomden plays keyboards and guitar and is a vocalist with the Analogues, a Dutch Beatles tribute band which performs music that the Beatles never played live. He was previously a member of the groups Rediver, Johan and Daryll-Ann.

Sir Tim Rice is a lyricist whose songs have featured in the hit musicals *Jesus Christ Superstar*, *Evita* and *Chess*, plus the films *Aladdin*, *Beauty and the Beast* and *The Lion King*. He was knighted in 1994 and has been awarded Oscar, Grammy, Emmy and Tony awards for his work.

David Roberts is the former editor of the *Guinness Book of Hit Singles & Albums* and also author of *Rock Atlas* – UK and US editions – and the Stephen Stills biography *Change Partners*.

Tom Robinson led the Tom Robinson Band in the 1970s when they had hits with '2-4-6-8 Motorway' and 'Rising Free'. After forming Sector 27, he went on to have a solo hit with 'War Baby' in 1983 and is now a regular broadcaster on BBC6 Music.

Contributors

Paul Sexton is a British journalist and broadcaster who began writing about music for *Record Mirror* while still at school. He is a regular writer for *The Sunday Times* and has written and produced music documentaries for BBC Radio 2.

Brian Southall worked for both *Melody Maker* and *Disc* before joining A&M Records in 1973. He moved to EMI in 1974 and stayed for 15 years before moving on to Warner Music. He has written 20 books about music, including the official history of Abbey Road and 50th anniversary titles about the albums *Sgt. Pepper* and *The Beatles*.

Chris Thomas is an acclaimed BRIT award-winning producer who joined Sir George Martin at AIR Studios in 1968 and worked on both *The Beatles* and *Abbey Road*. He was 'mixing supervisor' on Pink Floyd's *Dark Side of the Moon* and has produced Roxy Music, Elton John and Paul McCartney.

Left: The Beatles fly in for another concert tour and Ringo Starr captures the moment on camera.

Ken Townsend began at Abbey Road Studios in 1950 – on the same day as George Martin – and worked as a sound engineer on many Beatles recordings throughout the 1960s. He became General Manager of Abbey Road and retired in 1992, after 42 years with EMI, as Chairman of the Studio Group.

Johnny Walker began broadcasting on pirate radio stations Swinging Radio England and Radio Caroline before joining BBC Radio 1 in 1969. In 1976 he moved to America and worked in US radio before returning to Radio 1 in 1987. He currently presents *Sounds of the 70s* on BBC Radio 2.

Bart van Poppel is vocalist, bassist and keyboard player with the Analogues, in addition to producing the five-piece group's stage shows and recordings. He co-founded the Beatles tribute band in 2014 after playing with acts such as Shine and Tambourine.

Kenneth Womack is Dean of the Wayne D. McMurray School of Humanities and Social Sciences at Monmouth University, where he also serves as Professor of English. He is the author or editor of numerous books about the Beatles and a two-volume biography of Beatles producer George Martin

Opposite: The Beatles stop off for a cup of tea at Pier Head, Liverpool, February 1, 1963.

The Bootleg Beatles

Gordon Elsmore has portrayed Ringo Starr in the Bootleg Beatles since 2016. Before that he was in the tribute act Paperback Beatles and the West End production of the Beatles-inspired musical *Let It Be*.

Stephen Hill has played the role of George Harrison in the Bootleg Beatles since 2014. He previously toured with Gerry and the Pacemakers and appeared in the West End production of the musical *Let It Be*.

Tyson Kelly joined the Bootleg Beatles in 2018 as a new John Lennon after previously performing in *Sessions*, a show which recreated the Beatles' *Abbey Road* recordings and was performed at London's Royal Albert Hall in 2016.

Stephen White has been Paul McCartney in the Bootleg Beatles, who were formed in 1980, since 2012. He has played with a number of Beatles tribute acts, including shows at the Liverpool Cavern, and was part of the Bootleg Beatles performance at Glastonbury in 2013.

Introduction

There are 12 albums – yes, just a dozen – listed as official, original UK Beatles albums released during their time as the world's most popular, successful and creative group of musicians.

Between 1963 and 1970 John Lennon, Paul McCartney, George Harrison and Ringo Starr dominated the airwaves and the charts with their music. For those of us who were around back then it was a magical, unforgettable time in our lives. From *Please Please Me* to *Let It Be* they set records and standards that arguably will never be broken or bettered.

I was 15 when I first came across the Beatles; and little did I know back then that I would one day work on their recordings. From 1974 to 1989, I worked at EMI (both Records and Music) as press chief, marketing manager, head of radio and TV promotion and director of corporate communications. That work brought me into direct contact with the three ex-Beatles who remained in Britain after the group's break-up and continued to record for EMI as solo artists.

There was George Harrison's *Extra Texture* album and *The Best of George Harrison* collection; Ringo Starr's *Goodnight Vienna* and his *Blast From Your Past* compilation; and 10 titles from Paul McCartney (including some with Wings and some as Wings) stretching from *Venus and Mars* through to *Give My Regards to Broad Street*.

That of course leaves John Lennon, who moved to New York in 1971 and never returned to the UK before his murder in 1980. During that time we released *Walls and Bridges*, *Rock 'n' Roll* and the compilation *Shaved Fish*. Contact with Lennon usually came in the form of telexes and postcards, which told us what we should be doing and where we had gone wrong, since none of those albums ever topped the UK chart.

These were memorable moments for someone who bought and treasured everything the Beatles ever recorded and released. As an added bonus, I also came into regular contact with producer George Martin and was able to visit Abbey Road Studios regularly – I even ended up writing its official history.

During that time at EMI, I had offices in Manchester Square where, on an almost daily basis, I would walk across the landing where the first Beatles album cover was photographed. More than once I held impromptu meetings with an artist, manager or colleague while nonchalantly propped against the same stairwell bannister the band were pictured leaning over in 1963.

So while I didn't work on any of the Beatles' dozen official album releases, I was a member of the team involved in (and criticized for) the release of *Rock 'n' Roll Music* in 1976. It was described by George Martin as a "troubled" collection of earlier recordings and featured a cover that was criticized (and rightly so, in my opinion) by the Beatles.

Then we pulled together the live recordings of two of the group's performances in Los Angeles, from 1964 and 1965 to create the album *The Beatles at the Hollywood Bowl*, which was surprisingly well received when it came out in 1977. Both these albums were released after the Beatles' final contract with EMI expired in 1976, meaning that the group had no real influence over what we did with their music.

Taking full advantage of this newfound opportunity to repackage the Beatles' rich catalogue, we continued with *Love Songs*, *Rarities*, *Beatles Ballads*, *Reel Music* and *20 Greatest Hits*.

After that I moved on to an international role within EMI and was no longer involved in the UK company's releases, although I was around to observe the issues involved in the company's eventual release of the Beatles Catalogue in its first CD format in 1987.

Previous pages: The Beatles posed for a session with French photographer Jean-Marie Perier in 1967, the year of *Sgt. Pepper*.

Opposite: The fans always turned out in their thousands at airports to either greet the Beatles when they arrived home or to wave them off on tour.

The album was recorded on February 11, 1963 in EMI's Abbey Road Studios with George Martin as producer and Norman Smith as engineer. (Both of them had been in the studio when the Beatles, with Pete Best on drums, performed their original audition for Martin on June 6, 1962.)

Ten tracks were completed (with Ringo Starr on drums) between 10 a.m. and around midnight – including Lennon's extraordinary version of 'Twist And Shout', which took the session past the usual 10 p.m. closing time – and they were added to the Beatles' two hit singles 'Love Me Do'/'P.S. I Love You' and 'Please Please Me'/'Ask Me Why', which had been recorded in September and November 1962.

In the weeks leading up to the album's release there was a suggestion from George Martin that the Beatles' debut collection should be called *Off the Beatles Track* and Paul McCartney even went as far as producing some illustrations to go with the that title.

However, everybody eventually agreed that the album should be named after the group's

bestselling single to date, although the cover photograph on the Beatles' first album was not George Martin's original idea. As an honorary fellow of the Zoological Society of London, which owns London Zoo, Martin thought it might be good publicity for the zoo to have the Beatles pose outside the insect house for the cover photograph. When the Society turned him down, Martin called up the famous portrait photographer Angus McBean, who had taken cover shots for Cliff Richard's early albums. He decided to photograph the Beatles looking down over the stairwell inside EMI's London headquarters.

Years later, Martin said: "We rang up the legendary theatre photographer Angus McBean, and bingo, he came round and did it there and then. It was done in an almighty rush, like the music. The sleeve notes for the album were written by the Beatles' press officer Tony Barrow, who says, "People inside and outside the record industry expressed tremendous interest in the new vocal and instrumental sounds the Beatles had introduced."

Please Please Me entered the charts on April 6, 1963 and knocked Cliff and the Shadows off the top spot on May 11, spending the next 30 weeks at Number One and a total of 70 in the charts. And there was more to come.

Please Please Me
released March 22, 1963

I Saw Her Standing There
Misery
Anna (Go To Him)
Chains
Boys
Ask Me Why
Please Please Me
Love Me Do
P.S. I Love You
Baby It's You
Do You Want To Know a Secret
A Taste Of Honey
There's A Place
Twist And Shout

Reached #1 in the UK album chart and #5 in both France and Germany.

Previous pages: (L–R) George Harrison, Ringo Starr, Paul McCartney and John Lennon pose in the car park at Abbey Road Studios.

Left: (L–R) John Lennon, Paul McCartney and George Harrison inside Abbey Road's famous Studio 2.

Opposite: The Beatles captured out and about in London for *Boyfriend* magazine. The photo third down in the middle row became the cover of their *Twist And Shout* EP.

Moody Blues and Wings – who used to date my girlfriend Jenny.

"After what seemed an age, the Beatles finally came on. The first song they kicked into was 'I Saw Her Standing There'. The amount of screaming and the hysteria and the energy and the excitement was like nothing I have ever experienced since.

"My girlfriend loved the Beatles and I can't remember whether I bought it for her or she bought it for me but there was a tremendous excitement about getting the Beatles' *Please Please Me* album, with all those great songs on it.

"I've always been a fan of Motown so to get those songs on there … and I loved the Cookies' 'Chains'. I really liked the covers [the Beatles] did. It was the first British album of its type – a great pop album with covers and their own songs. *Please Please Me* is a real classic of its time.

"Seeing them on TV doing songs from *Please Please Me* inspired me – the freshness and the energy and the fact that they upset lots of adults with their raucous music and long hair, grown-ups hating it just made us love it more. I thought, here are four ordinary guys from Liverpool and they're creating all this excitement and managing to do something that we never thought young people could do. That gave me the impetus to think about my life and not to settle for the conventional life that was planned out for me."

Ray Connolly

"I was at the LSE in London and my girlfriend (now wife) wrote to me to say that she had been to see this group called the Beatles and then I heard *Please Please Me* in a house in Grimsby … and it all hit me like a brick as I realized they were the same blokes my wife had seen.

"It is a great album – there are some great tracks on it and you couldn't work out who was the lead singer, which was completely new."

Gordon Elsmore

"*Please Please Me* was the Beatles in their rawest form. When you listen to that album you're hearing a band that had done so much and managed to craft their own sort of sound. You hear that on that album; there's no fudging of any kind – it's just them and you can hear how they work together. That's the original sound of the Beatles as far as I'm concerned.

"'Twist And Shout' was the song that really got me going. I don't think John Lennon ever sounded

the same again in any other period of the Beatles – he was a man singing for his life with one take in him. He knew what he had to do to complete the task – it is an amazing vocal performance.

"I think 'Boys' is Ringo's best moment – he's singing and playing at the same time and it's an incredible vocal and drumming performance – you can really hear him going for it.

"It kicked off the career of the Beatles and when you hear *Please Please Me* you are hearing all the work that happened before then, which was quite considerable with the Cavern and Hamburg. They were massively professional by the time they made the album and in just 10 to 12 hours they made an album that sounded like they'd been working on it for a long, long time."

Tim Rice

"I think it's probably true that *Please Please Me* did change people's lives; it made an enormous impact even though we hadn't a clue what was coming. In fact the first two albums were enormously influential as whereever you went when I was 18 or 19 years old it was on at every party and you learnt every track and the order they were in.

"It was also an introduction for a lot of people to a lot of American music such as Arthur Alexander, and to have two Shirelles tracks ('Baby It's You' and 'Boys') on the first album was extraordinary. If you asked which one influenced my life most, I would definitely have to say *Please Please Me* – and then I ended up working at EMI where the front cover was photographed.

"I was already a Beatles fan but when I heard 'Please Please Me' the single I didn't think 'this is the change' but when the album came out a bit later it was at that point that you thought 'hello, this definitely is a change, something new'. It had such a lot of energy.

"I once spoke in a debate in which the motion was that 'She was just seventeen, you know what I mean' – from 'I Saw Her Standing There' – are the two greatest lines in the English language. I was saying that they were – even though they were up against Shakespeare, Byron and Dickens – and one of the brilliant things is that within the first two lines of the first Beatles album there is 'she' – third person; 'you' – second person; 'I' – first person, which is a brilliant run through of English grammar in the first sentence."

Opposite: The Beatles join the police on duty after their concert in Birmingham in November 1963.

Overleaf: The Beatles (L–R), Paul McCartney, George Harrison, Ringo Starr and John Lennon sign music publishing papers for Northern Songs co-founder Dick James (extreme left).

- On February 11, 2013 BBC Radio 6 Music celebrated the 50th anniversary of the recording of *Please Please Me* by broadcasting a recreation of the original session in Abbey Road Studios with guest artists performing the songs from the album. Presenter Stuart Maconie hosted the show and said, "It's not the best Beatles album. But it's the first Beatles album. It's the first album of the rock era really. That's what people forget, it was all about singles and it was the first self-contained album and it did change the whole rock era."

- Simply Red lead singer Mick Hucknall, who sang 'Anna (Go to Him)' during the session, said, "Pinch me! When I bought my first Beatles album when I was 11 and was sat [listening to it] in my dad's kitchen, if you were to tell me that I'd be standing in Abbey Road [Studios], paying tribute to the Beatles, who would have believed you?"

- George Martin (*All You Need is Ears*): "After the success of *Please Please Me* (single) I realized that we had to act very fast to get a long-playing album on the market if we were to cash in in on what we had already achieved. I knew their repertoire from the Cavern and I called the boys down to the studio and said, 'Right, what you're going to do now, today, straight away, is play me this selection of things I've chosen from what you do in the Cavern.' All we did was to reproduce the Cavern performance in the comparative calm of the studio."

- Norman Smith, Beatles engineer and later producer of Pink Floyd: "They [the Beatles] brought in loads and loads of records from Liverpool to show what sounds they wanted. They were so aware of what was going on in America, where they most definitely were ahead of us in pop production. They brought in things like Carl Perkins and a lot of Motown stuff."

- Long-time Beatles engineer Geoff Emerick was tape operator on February 22, 1963, the day overdubs were done for the album. He wrote in *Here, There and Everywhere*: "None of the Beatles were present – they were out on tour – but it was a fabulous session nonetheless, if only for the fact that I got an advance listen of many of the album tracks. I was completely blown away. It was the freshest music I'd heard, and I remember raving to my mates about it afterwards."

What the Beatles Said

"We did that first album in a day – 14 hours I think it was. We never took much longer than a day. George Martin's contribution to our songs was quite a big one. George was in there quite heavily from the beginning."
Paul McCartney (*Abbey Road*)

"The *Please Please Me* cover is crap but at that time it hadn't mattered. We hadn't even thought it was lousy probably because we were so pleased to be on a record."
George Harrison (*The Beatles Anthology*)

"The first [album] we just did as a 'group'; we went in and played and they put it on tape and we went. They remixed it, they did everything to it."
John Lennon (*The Beatles Anthology*)

Left: The Beatles backstage at the Cavern Club in Liverpool. They played their last show there in August 1963.

Previous pages: It's the Beatles, but in the wrong order – Ringo, John, Paul and George.

What the Critics Said

"Fourteen exciting tracks with the instrumental drive that has put this Liverpool group way up on top in a very short time."

New Musical Express, April 1963

"... their debut Parlophone LP. It bids [sic] well for the future. This Liverpool group is one up on the batch of pop groups in the country for their combination of top-class twang and exciting, all-stops-out vocal works links into a formidably commercial sound."

Melody Maker, April 1963

"These boys look good, sound good and ARE good – very good. Their sheer professionalism reminds one of the bluesy coloured groups which abound on the other side of the Atlantic, which is to say they specialize in a form of group singing far above the limitations of the majority of British vocal teams."

Richard Attenborough, EMI's *Record Mail* newspaper, May 1963

"'One, Two, Three Four!' Paul McCartney's shouted count launches the Beatles into the clipped, thrilling

Opposite: John Lennon picks away at his guitar.

Below: Beatles manager Brian Epstein in a backstage meeting.

dancehall belter 'I Saw Her Standing There'. After everything that has been said about the band, imbuing them with an almost supernatural hue, it is always amazing to hear them on their debut, just a sharp, fresh, rock 'n' roll band, the savage young Beatles."

"Recorded in one 12-hour session on two-track tape, the sheer accomplishment of their tight, syncopated playing and perfect harmony singing is astonishing to behold. I doubt there is a young group who could do anything comparable today.

"There are just five original Lennon and McCartney songs, but the way the adrenalized, proto-Beatlemania rocker 'Please Please Me' rips out of their rhythm and blues roots into a hot, new pop form shows what the world has in

store. Other originals include some of their most awkward and naive songs ('Ask Me Why' and 'P.S. I Love You'), yet they nonetheless display ambition in their chords and harmonies.

"This slightly rough and ready debut is as close as we can get to their early live set. The range of their tastes is reflected in their penchant for slightly saccharine ballads, melody already as important to them as the sharp rhythmic groove and tough rock sensibility of the utterly sensational, snotty version of 'Twist and Shout', which features a fearless lead vocal from Lennon that defined the way British rock singers would approach the mike ever after."

Neil McCormick, *Daily Telegraph*, September 2009

Above: The Beatles and producer George Martin pose with a silver disc for the single 'Please Please Me'.

Opposite: December 1963 and the Beatles were in Birmingham for the *Thank Your Lucky Stars* TV show.

1963
With The Beatles

Previous pages: John Lennon finds time to relax between recording and touring.

Left: The Beatles rehearsing their routine for the 1963 Royal Command Performance.

By the time the Beatles began work on their second album, they had recorded both their Number One hit singles 'From Me to You' and 'She Loves You' and played a handful of dates around the UK including six nights at Margate Winter Gardens.

The first four tracks for *With The Beatles* – 'You Really Got a Hold on Me', 'Money', 'Devil in Her Heart' and 'Till There Was You' – were recorded on July 18, 1963. Work on the album resumed in September in-between live performances in Blackpool, the Channel Islands, Llandudno. Torquay, Worcester, Croydon and at London's Royal Albert Hall. The Beatles also played their last ever gig at the Cavern in Liverpool on August 3.

The album was completed in sessions between September 18 and October 23, when 'I Wanna Be Your Man', 'Little Child' and 'Hold Me Tight' were finished with George Martin and engineer Norman Smith overseeing the sessions. Once again there were eight songs written by the

Beatles among the 14 titles; but this time there was a difference.

George Harrison appeared as a composer for the first time as 'Don't Bother Me' sat alongside seven original songs by John Lennon and Paul McCartney and six covers – three of them from the Detroit-based Tamla Motown label.

In his role as the Beatles' resident writer of sleeve notes Tony Barrow explained that the eight original Beatles compositions sat alongside "a batch of 'personal choice' pieces selected from the recorded repertoire of the American R&B artists they admire most."

While George Martin had been influential in the choice of photographer for the cover of the group's first album, it was down to their manager Brian Epstein to step in with a suggestion for the follow-up. He had seen the work of British photographer Robert Freeman and been particularly impressed with his work with jazz musicians such as John Coltrane and Dizzy Gillespie.

After sending a portfolio of his work to the Beatles during their six-night stay in Llandudno playing the Odeon cinema, Freeman assembled the band at the Palace Court Hotel in Bournemouth on August 22, during another six-night residency, to

With The Beatles

Released November 22, 1963 (Parlophone)

It Won't Be Long

All I've Got To Do

All My Loving

Don't Bother Me

Little Child

Till There Was You

Please Mister Postman

Roll Over Beethoven

Hold Me Tight

You Really Got A Hold On Me

I Wanna be Your Man

Devil In Her Heart

Not a Second Time

Money

Reached #1 in the UK and in Germany but peaked at #5 in France (again).

pose for the iconic black and white portrait that would become the cover.

Looking back, Freeman, who was paid £75 for his work, recalled, "They had to fit in the square format of the cover so rather than have them all in a line, I put Ringo in the bottom right corner, since he was the last to join the group. He was also the shortest."

Released eight months to the day after the *Please Please Me* album, *With The Beatles* arrived with advance orders of 300,000 and replaced *Please Please Me* at Number One in the UK album chart on December 7, 1963 – after a stay of around seven months.

The Beatles' second album topped the chart for the next 21 weeks, passing the half-million sales mark and even appearing in the UK singles chart (which didn't differentiate about the size of bestselling records back then), before handing over the top spot to arch rivals The Rolling Stones ... but not for long.

Below: (L–R) John Lennon, Paul McCartney, George Harrison and Ringo Starr take time out for tea.

Gered Mankowitz

"To be honest I have to choose *With The Beatles* because of the sleeve. I always liked Robert Freeman's work and I think what he did with the Beatles throughout the sixties was fantastic. But *With The Beatles* had a particular impact.

"It was their second album and after the first Angus McBean shot in EMI, which wasn't a great cover, it seemed to have style and subtlety and they looked great and it was also a very clever way of maintaining the uniform without the little suits.

"Being a black and white sleeve was funny and stunning. It influenced me in the sense that one could suddenly think about a grainy, gritty, moody black and white picture as a cover image. The other thing I like about it is that when I worked with Robert – we had shows together – and I said to him that I'd always loved *With The Beatles*, he replied, 'The Beatles – they were bloody lucky to get me'.

"He was a great a great photographer and that was a particularly strong, powerful and, in its own quiet way, revolutionary cover – a beautiful, simple solution. It was a big change.

"Musically it was a transitional album I suppose – a lot of covers, a few originals. I thought it was a good album, considering that the second album is always difficult for most acts. There were some good tracks and some good covers – I liked it very much. There's a rawness and authenticity and naturalness to the album.

"I was seventeen that year and I think I went out and bought it although the vinyl I have in my collection is actually my wife's copy – it has her name on it. There was great excitement attached with every album they brought out and the sleeve was an important part of the whole thing; it was what you saw first.

"This sleeve photo is arguably the most iconic of the Beatles ever taken, as well as being one of the sixties' most defining images."

Right: The Beatles relax before a Christmas concert in 1963.

Tom Robinson

"*With The Beatles* followed and I got that for Christmas in 1963 as a present because I couldn't afford it. And so that winter I finally caught up with *With The Beatles*. You get those two albums and then you get *A Hard Day's Night* – 'Oh my God one, two, three ...' At that point you're hooked."

Stephen Hill

"I love all the Beatles albums – even *Yellow Submarine* – but it has to be *With The Beatles* mainly because of John Lennon's vocals; he doesn't seem to sound on any other record like he does on this one – he's pushing himself.

"'It Won't Be Long' is just a kick in the face to start it off and then it's into 'All I've Got To Do', which is a nice ballad, so he's showing off two sides of his voice straight away. I love the way Lennon sings, and even though I portray George with the Bootlegs, it's all about Lennon on this album for me and he just nails every single song on it.

"I've heard Lennon talking about songs on the album like 'Not A Second Time' and 'Little Child' and he kinda passes these songs off as throwaway songs but for me they are just wicked, wicked pop songs. The whole band is on form on the album.

"For me this album is the bridge between the first album and the real superstardom that came with *A Hard' Day's Night*, which was when they went supersonic, so this is a real transition album for the Beatles.

"The cover picture – with George's ears sticking out - is the reason why on stage when I'm George I always tuck a bit of sponge or tissue under the wig cap to push my ears out when we're doing stuff from that period."

Glen Matlock

"Their version of 'Money' is great. 'Roll Over Beethoven' is good too and I'm a sucker for that Little Richard vocal thing that McCartney does so well. I like the Beatles when they are really rocking."

Tony Bramwell

"I am painfully aware of the many hundreds of brilliant recordings that the Beatles made and that *Revolver* and *Sgt. Pepper* are practically sanctified as masterpieces! But I must say my favourite recordings are probably *Please Please Me* and *With The Beatles*.

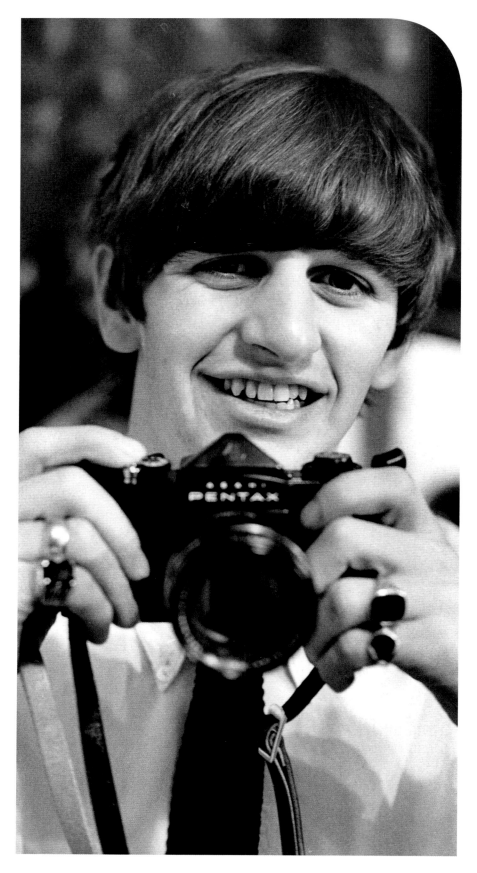

"These records capture a more exciting stage of the band's career. Unfortunately not many people ever witnessed the Beatles when they were an exciting rock band playing several hours per lunchtime and at evening and all-night gigs. After the spring of 1963 the concerts were only a maximum of 35 minutes, consisting of the hits.

"These early albums do capture some of the energy that they had as a remarkably great band of musicians and vocalists, and you can hear the influences that combined to manufacture the Beatles' sound. The amazing mixture of pop classics, movie songs, music hall, rhythm and blues, rock 'n' roll, comedy, harmony songs, country songs, folk songs and girl group offerings – plus a few of their own compositions! They were just amazing as a live act."

Above: The Beatles prepare for a gig at the Cavern in 1963.

Left: Paul McCartney practises his keyboard skills.

Opposite: Ringo Starr, ever the keen amateur photographer.

"For some reason I was asked to assist George [Martin] and Norman [Smith] for the album's editing and mixing. As I sat in the control room listening to the tracks I was amazed at how much the Beatles had improved since their debut album, in terms of confidence and musicianship and their singing. All in all, there was a great spirit about that album."
Geoff Emerick

"The Beatles were totally influential for me, particularly *With The Beatles* – that one really got me. I was about 14 and had a group myself, The Outer Limits, but we were more into the Stones because their stuff was easier to play. The Beatles were always more complicated.
　　"A lot of things I learnt as a producer came from listening very closely to Beatles records, and you only have to spend ten minutes with Paul to understand why they were so good."
Trevor Horn (ex-member of Buggles and producer of Frankie Goes To Hollywood, Pet Shop Boys and Paul McCartney), *Daily Telegraph*

1964

A Hard Day's Night

After the Beatles finished work on their second album in October 1963, they set off on a tour of the UK, which ran from the start of November to mid-December. They performed their Christmas show for 16 nights at London's Finsbury Park Astoria, played 20 days (and nights) at the Paris Olympia theatre and finally visited America – for concerts and TV appearances – in February 1964.

While they were in Paris during January 1964, the Beatles recorded German language versions of their UK number one hits, 'I Want to Hold Your Hand' ('Komm, Gib Mir Deine Hand') and 'She Loves You' ('Sie Liebt Dich'). On the same day, January 29, they completed 'Can't Buy Me Love' in just four takes.

John, Paul, George and Ringo eventually returned to Abbey Road Studios on February 25, 1964 to start work on an album destined to be the soundtrack to their first film, set to start shooting on March 2. They began with the songs 'You Can't Do That' and 'And I Love Her' and then completed the album's opening track and the film's title song in one day on April 16.

In just eight recording sessions – the final one on June 2 – the Beatles completed the seven tracks that would be used in the film, plus the extra six for Side Two of the album. A *Hard Day's Night* was the first album to feature songs all written by Lennon and McCartney.

With a budget of £200,000, filming A *Hard Day's Night* began with a scene showing the Beatles on a train leaving Paddington Station's platform 5 and continued around London for two months. The finished movie was premiered at the London Pavilion on July 6 with Princess Margaret and her husband, Lord Snowdon, in the audience. Four days later 200,000 fans filled the streets of Liverpool when the Beatles returned home for the film's northern premiere.

The film was released worldwide with foreign language versions appearing in Italy (*Tutti Per Uno – All For One*), Germany (*Yeah, Yeah, Yeah,*), France (*Quatre Garçons dans le Vent – Four Boys in the Wind*)), Finland (*Yeah! Yeah! Tässä Me Tulemme – Yeah! Yeah! Here We Come*) and Brazil (*Os Reis do Ié-Ié-Ié – The Kings of Yeah, Yeah,Yeah*).

The album's artwork was once again the work of photographer Robert Freeman although, oddly,

A Hard Day's Night
Released July 10, 1964 (Parlophone)

A Hard Day's Night
I Should Have Known Better
If I Fell
I'm Happy Just To Dance With You
And I Love Her
Tell Me Why
Can't Buy Me Love
Any Time At All
I'll Cry Instead
Things We Said Today
You Can't Do That
I'll Be Back

Reached #1 in the UK, Australia and Germany. In *Q* magazine's 2000 listing of the 100 Greatest British Albums Ever, *A Hard Day's Night* was listed at #5 while in *Rolling Stone*'s listing of the 25 Greatest Soundtracks of All Time it came in at #4.

Previous pages: The Beatles took to the stage in America for the first time at the Washington Coliseum on February 11, 1964.

Left: (L–R) Paul McCartney, George Harrison, Ringo Starr and John Lennon dip their toes in the sea in Miami in 1964.

Opposite: The Beatles pose with balloons, beers and a few party snacks to promote the BBC World Service.

he was never credited on the album sleeve. He gathered the Beatles in his London studio for the cover shoot, which featured the four pulling different facial expressions in each shot.

Tony Barrow's album sleeve notes recalled a piano being moved into the Beatles' suite at the George V Hotel in Paris during their January stay as John and Paul "began to compile a collection of new compositions for the soundtrack". He described the songs on Side One (and on the soundtrack) as "the magnificent seven". "When you listen to the second side of this record you will agree that it would have been a pity to cast aside such a fabulous set of songs solely because they couldn't be fitted into the structure of A *Hard Day's Night*."

Already pronounced by NME in January 1964 to be the UK's top record-selling act the previous year, the Beatles entered the UK album chart with A *Hard Day's Night* on July 18, 1964. It hit the top spot a week later, deposing the Rolling Stones. Emulating its predecessor *With The Beatles*, the group's third album remained at Number One for 21 weeks before another Fab Four title arrived.

Opposite: American fans and police wait for The Beatles outside New York's Plaza Hotel in 1964.

Left: (L–R) George Harrison, Paul McCartney and John Lennon take in the sights of Paris in January 1964.

Below: The Beatles filmed the TV special *Around the Beatles* in April 1964 and it was broadcast a month later.

Brian Southall

"Which came first, the album or the film? That's a question I couldn't answer when it came down to my own experience of A Hard Day's Night. We all know that the movie was premiered in London on July 6, 1964 and that the album came out four days later on July 10, but I had trouble remembering which of them came into my life first.

"My 17th birthday was on July 21 so it's possible that the album was a present. And as the film didn't go on general release for probably at least another week or fortnight, I may not have got round to seeing it at my local cinema until after the album's release date. On the back of a little research at my local records office, I have established that the movie didn't actually open at my local Odeon until Sunday August 9.

"My local paper (which I joined a couple of years later) carried a brief preview of the Beatles' offering, which said, "The long-awaited advent of the Beatles into the world of film. A highly amusing insight into the everyday lives of the four most popular entertainers in the world today. Too good to miss."

"So it was almost certain that the album came into my life first; but it didn't really matter as I greeted both the record and the film with equal delight, from George Harrison's extraordinary guitar chord opening the title track to the film's final scene as the Beatles flew off in a helicopter – with 'A Hard Day's Night' playing over the credits.

"For a teenager the film was a riotous, rebellious bonanza as our new pop heroes did their thing and ran riot around London. It would be another seven or eight years before I actually went to Paddington station where the opening scenes were set but not actually filmed.

"In fact it wasn't important to know where the scenes were shot or what guitars the boys in the band were playing – those of us who weren't

Above: The Beatles met the American media at a press conference in New York in February 1964.

Opposite above: The Beatles on location around London filming *A Hard Day's Night* in March 1964.

Opposite below: George Harrison signs autographs for a couple of fans.

experts or guitarists didn't really know the difference or indeed care. It was the fact that the Beatles played the music that back then was on Side One of an LP; and when I came to play it at home, I had images to go with each tune.

"The first side of the album remains a joy; and not just because of the two chart-topping tunes 'A Hard Day's Night' and 'Can't Buy Me Love' – the fourth and fifth of the group's long list of Number Ones – which opened and closed Side One. The other five tracks, together with the six on Side Two (which weren't included in the film; that was where the album had the advantage) showed – even to an ardent fan who would have lapped up anything the Fab Four did – a new maturity that was to lead to even greater delights.

"I revelled in the tomfoolery of the film while at the same time cherishing my original copy of the album, which I could play and play and play again. It was mine: the third LP in my growing Beatles collection."

Tom Robinson

"A *Hard Day's Night* was really good – they pulled that out of the bag. No covers, all original songs, great movie and songs to match plus two singles on the album – so well done them.

  "You get those three albums and that certifies their place in the firmament; plus those monster singles that came early on. Despite the fact that we're talking about their albums, they were really still a singles band at that time."

Ray Connolly

"A *Hard Day's Night* has some great songs on it. I saw it soon after it came out at the London Pavilion where it was premiered. It was a great little film with some great songs – mainly by John."

Glen Matlock

"I saw the movie and their songwriting had really come through by then. They had kind of amalgamated and merged all their influences and defined their own style. Their third album in just over a year so they really packed 'em in back then."

Ken Townsend

"Up to around 1964 the Beatles were paid session fees as members of the Musicians' Union. I think it was £5.10s for two hours and £7 or something for three hours. They were paid these fees at Abbey Road – sometimes I gave them the money in envelopes. But probably after *A Hard Day's Night* they were paid nothing as session musicians and just got their EMI royalty – whatever it was by then."

Left: The Beatles faced over 14,000 fans when they played at the Seattle Coliseum in August 1964.

Below: Screaming fans greeted the Beatles wherever they went in the world.

Overleaf: The band get to know US TV host Ed Sullivan (centre) in New York in February 1964.

- Tony Barrow (*John, Paul, George, Ringo & Me*): "The only innovation in the film (for those few souls who noticed) was the use by George of a Rickenbacker 12-string guitar, a radically new and much sought-after instrument at the time, and the earliest influence of Bob Dylan on John Lennon's work.

  "But the Fab Four's musical output stood little chance of making more substantial creative progress when most of their days were spent scampering from country to country, from job to job. Thankfully the Lennon and McCartney combination often worked well under pressure and the numbers written for the soundtrack of *A Hard Day's Night* included several that were special even by the dynamic duo's high standards. John and Paul never turned out soundtrack songs as dire as some of those encountered in Elvis Presley's screen vehicles."

- George Martin (*The Complete Beatles Recording Sessions*): "We knew the song 'A Hard Day's Night' would open both the film and the soundtrack LP, so we wanted a particularly strong and effective beginning. The strident guitar chord was the perfect launch."

- Norman Smith, engineer on Beatles sessions from 1962 to 1965: "We had done the first Beatles album in one day but by the time we did the third LP we had four tracks and [the band] were just as interested as the rest of us in creating new sounds.

  "They also changed the discipline of the place. They worked exactly when they wanted to work and brought absolute chaos to Abbey Road. They rehearsed and practised routines in there and occasionally – though rarely – wrote songs in the studio. Very often Paul would have a song and the first time the others heard it was in the studio and this happened with John as well. They would swap ideas with each other and get the song exactly right before they recorded it."

- Helen Shapiro: "One day when I'd finished in Studio One, I went to the control room in Studio Two to see the Beatles when they were doing 'Can't Buy Me Love'. They insisted on playing it back to me and then Ringo had to go down and put on extra cymbals over the top – apparently this was something he did quite often on their records.

  "They were the first artists to go into the studio and say, 'I've not quite finished yet' and then rehearse a song and add things to it. This effectively put an end to the old concept of three-hour sessions."

- Björn Borg (*Liverpool Echo*, September 2009)" "*A Hard Day's Night* is my favourite Beatles album and [has on it] my two favourite Beatles songs ever – 'If I Fell' and 'And I Love Her' – neither of which were singles."

- Geoff Emerick (*Here, There and Everywhere*): "All in all I enjoyed *A Hard Day's Night*. To me it was a definite improvement over previous rock 'n' roll movies. The Beatles themselves were portrayed as four stereotypes in the movie and I remember sitting there thinking to myself, 'They're not really like that'."

What the Beatles Said

"So *A Hard Day's Night* was like a day in the life; or really, two days and two nights of our life. We'd go to the recording studio then go to the TV studio. All the things that happened to us were put in."

Ringo Starr (*The Beatles Anthology*)

"Usually John and I would sit down and if we thought of something we'd write a song about it. But Walter Shenson [the film's producer] asked John and me if we'd write a song especially for the opening and closing credits.

"We thought about 'A Hard Day's Night' – it sounded funny at the time but after a bit we got the idea of saying it had been a hard day's night and we'd been working all the days and get back to a girl and everything's fine ... And we turned it into one of those songs."

Paul McCartney (*The Beatles Anthology*)

"Paul and I enjoyed writing the music for the film. There were times when we honestly thought we'd never get the time to write all the material."

John Lennon (*The Beatles Anthology*)

"We'd loved *The Girl Can't Help It* [an American rock 'n' roll film from 1956 starring Little Richard, Eddie Cochran, Gene Vincent and Jayne Mansfield] and we knew you could make a rock 'n' roll film. We'd seen those little American productions and, although they were low budget and not very good, they did have music and we always went to see them. So we wanted to be in one but we wanted be in a good one."

Paul McCartney (*The Beatles Anthology*)

Opposite left, above: Two Beatles take cover in a photo booth during the filming of *A Hard Day's Night*.

Opposite left, below: Paul McCartney in disguise during filming in London.

Above: John Lennon hated wearing glasses but sometimes it was necessary.

Opposite right: George Harrison's reading is interrupted by a phone call.

What the Critics Said

"The Beatles come through with flying colours. Whereas many pop stars sound unreal and even horrible when given lines in films, the Beatles really punch them over — and they look good throughout. Their on-beat singing is terrific."

Andy Gray, *NME*

"As crazily inconsequential, as endearingly insolent, as infectiously pleased with themselves — as funny as the Marx Brothers."

Cecil Wilson, *Daily Mail*

"Right from the thunderous opening chord, *A Hard Day's Night* jumps into a typical day in the madcap life of the Beatles. John Lennon and Paul McCartney hit new highs with tunes like 'If I Fell'."

Rolling Stone, August 2013

Opposite above: George Harrison (right) gets set to write while Ringo Starr adjusts his camera as John Lennon and Paul McCartney look on.

Opposite below: The Beatles performing at Carnegie Hall in New York.

Below: World boxing champion Muhammad Ali poses with the Beatles in Miami Beach in 1964.

1964
Beatles For Sale

On Aug 11, 1964 — two months after the release of *A Hard Day's Night* — the Beatles went back into the studio to start work on their second "Christmas" album, following on from their November 1963 release of *With The Beatles*.

They began with 'Baby's in Black' and after sessions throughout September and October, completed the recording of *Beatles For Sale* on October 26 with 'Honey Don't' and 'What You're Doing'. The album features the only Buddy Holly song the Beatles ever recorded – 'Words of Love' – despite the fact that all four were huge fans of the Texan-born singer, who died in 1959, and included his numbers in their stage shows from the late 1950s through to 1962.

Just a week after starting work on their new album, the Beatles embarked on their first major tour of America. They played 25 concerts, from San Francisco on August 19 to New York on September 20, and their August 23 show at the Hollywood Bowl in Los Angeles was recorded for a potential live album. This eventually came out in 1977.

Beatles For Sale

Released December 4, 1964 (Parlophone)

No Reply
I'm A Loser
Baby's In Black
Rock And Roll Music
I'll Follow The Sun
Mr. Moonlight
Medley (Kansas City/Hey, Hey, Hey, Hey)

Eight Days A Week
Words Of Love
Honey Don't
Every Little Thing
I Don't Want To Spoil The Party

What You're Doing
Everybody's Trying To Be My Baby

Reached #1 in the UK, Australia and Germany.

Back in the UK they began a tour on October 9, supported by the likes of Sounds Incorporated, Mary Wells and Tommy Quickly. They fitted in their two final recording sessions on days off between dates in Hull and Edinburgh, Brighton and Plymouth.

Beatles For Sale was the first Beatles album to come in a gatefold sleeve – one of the earliest examples of this sort of packaging being used in the UK. Once again, Robert Freeman produced the artwork, an autumnal scene shot in Hyde Park. Freeman climbed a tree to get the back cover shot.

Inside, the four Beatles appeared in front of a black and white montage featuring the film stars Victor Mature, Jayne Mansfield and Ian Carmichael, anticipating Peter Blake's famous *Sgt. Pepper* cover. The sleeve notes were written for the first time by Derek Taylor, the newly appointed personal assistant to Beatles' manager Brian Epstein, who had ghost-written Epstein's autobiography A *Cellarful of Noise.*

The Liverpool-born former *Daily Express* journalist Taylor wrote that *Beatles For Sale* included "eight new titles wrought by the

Previous pages: The Beatles go in the sea at Miami Beach in 1964.

Opposite above: The Beatles arrive in America for their first US tour in August 1964.

Opposite below: Over 8,000 fans saw the Beatles at the Washington Coliseum in February 1964.

Above: The Beatles rehearsing at the Deauville Hotel in Miami for their second appearance on *The Ed Sullivan Show.*

1965
Help!

The Beatles were away from Abbey Road – and all other recording studios – for an unprecedented three-and-a-half months between October 1964 and February 1965, when they returned to begin work on their fifth album.

They began work on 'Ticket To Ride' on February 15 and followed up with sessions over the next five days before jetting off to the Bahamas to begin work on their second feature film, called simply *Beatles Two* and then *Eight Arms to Hold You* before it became *Help!*

Directed and produced once again by Richard Lester and Walter Shenson for United Artists, and with a budget doubled to £400,000, filming continued in Austria and in England before wrapping on May 13.

Prior to the end of filming, the Beatles played their third successive NME Poll Winners Concert at Wembley's Empire Pool on April 11, where they performed five numbers before being presented with awards for World Vocal Group and British Vocal Group by American singer Tony Bennett.

Two days later they returned to the studio to record the track that would be used to introduce the new film and album. 'Help!' – described by Lennon as his first "message" number – was completed in 12 takes on the evening of April 13, and one more session was fitted in on May 10.

The final recordings of the album *Help!* took place over four consecutive days in June. In the final three sessions on June 17, Ringo Starr's standard single contribution was recorded. 'Act Naturally' became the last cover version the Beatles would record for four years.

Previous pages: (L–R) John Lennon, Paul McCartney, Ringo Starr and George Harrison on the slopes of the Austrian Alps filming *Help!*.

Opposite: John Lennon adopts a thoughtful expression during the filming for *Help!*.

Below: Ringo Starr (left) and John Lennon pose as next-door neighbours in Twickenham in a scene from *Help!*.

Help!

Released August 6 1965 (Parlophone)

Help!
The Night Before
You've Got To Hide Your Love Away
I Need You
Another Girl
You're Going To Lose That Girl
Ticket To Ride
Act Naturally
It's Only Love
You Like Me Too Much
Tell Me What You See
I've Just Seen A Face
Yesterday
Dizzy Miss Lizzy

Reached #1 in the UK, Australia and Germany, #5 in France. *Rolling Stone*'s 25 Greatest Soundtracks of All Time placed *Help!* at #1.

The new Beatles' film was premiered at the London Pavilion on July 29, once again with Princess Margaret and Lord Snowdon in attendance – as well as the 10,000 people who crammed into Leicester Square.

A week later the album *Help!* was released. As usual, the cover photograph was by Robert Freeman, who had a particular concept in mind for the sleeve. "I had the idea of semaphore spelling out the letters 'HELP'. But when we came to do the shot, the arrangement of the arms with those letters didn't look good. So we decided to improvise and ended up with the best graphic positioning of the arms." The end result had the Beatles spelling out the letters "NUJV".

Help! – with the seven original Beatles songs used in the film on Side One and a further seven tracks on Side Two – went straight to Number One in the UK album chart on August 14, replacing *The Sound of Music*. It stayed there for nine weeks until the famous soundtrack bounced back in October.

Opposite: (L–R) Paul McCartney, John Lennon and George Harrison filming *Help!* on Salisbury Plain in May 1965.

Above: Paul McCartney shares the news about the Beatles receiving MBEs.

Right: Paul McCartney and George Harrison get together in harmony.

Paul Sexton

"When I was younger, so much younger ... most of my lifetime ago, the Beatles first seized my heart not on disc, but on celluloid.

"Having two older sisters besotted with the Fabs – one of whom I still haven't forgiven for seeing them live at the Tooting Granada during the 1963 tour with Roy Orbison – I was subconsciously weaned on Merseybeat. But the point at which it all started to mean something was the day my mother improbably decided, even as I was the wide-eyed new bug in the 'infants', that I could be treated to my first visit to the cinema.

"No *Sound of Music* or *Mary Poppins* for me that day in 1965, although both were recent box office winners at the time. I got John, Paul, George and Ringo acting out a surreal Marx Brothers hallucination. I was five, and the film, of course, was *Help!*

"The nuances of the movie's endearingly bizarre plot were lost on me, but the image of four men doing semaphore in the snow was laser-locked, all the more so when I started to hear the accompanying album on our home lo-fi. My memory hasn't preserved exactly when I became aware of the *Help!* LP for the first time, but at least one sister would have been saving for it for weeks, so in all likelihood it was in the week of release.

"Later, like the entire world, I would be mesmerized by the group's ever-unfolding sonic sophistication. I specifically remember hearing the psychedelic breakdown in the middle of 'I Am The Walrus' and feeling as though I was suddenly wearing my brain backwards. A year later, when I started buying records, my first 45 was 'Hey Jude'. But for all that, *Help!* was already *my* Beatles album, and it still is.

"In an overview of their astounding oeuvre, it's the record in which the innocence of youth begins to be complemented by a more measured view of the world around them. But judged simply on its own merits, *Help!* is a magical synthesis of positive emotions, raucous energy and the life-affirming cohesion of four young men who wouldn't have wanted to be anywhere else in the world.

"The Beatles were navigating the uncharted profundity in pop music that they had invented, and what a breathtaking maturation that was. *Help!* arrived only eight months after *Beatles For Sale*, by which time all suspicions that their success might

be a passing whim had become a foolish memory. But while that lovable late 1964 set had them still partly in thrall to such heroes as Carl Perkins ('Honey Don't'), Buddy Holly ('Words of Love') and Chuck Berry ('Rock and Roll Music'), these new Beatles were now almost their own sovereign state of autonomous creativity.

"Only twice during this 14-chapter page-turner did *Help!* reach beyond the Lennon, McCartney and Harrison songbooks. Even then, it was for the sheer pleasure of introducing their impassioned audience to styles they might not have known. As a showcase for Ringo, they taught us the delights of country and western, covering Buck Owens's 1963

chart-topper 'Act Naturally' (written by Johnny Russell and Voni Morrison). Then they celebrated Larry Williams, another of their lesser-appreciated favourites from the early days of raw, R&B-fuelled rock 'n' roll, closing the LP with John's roaring remake of a 1958 gem from the Specialty Records archive, 'Dizzy Miss Lizzy'.

"By the time of that breathless send-off, *Help!* had offered a marvellous diversity of styles and sentiments. Here was Lennon, on a title track of superior melodiousness with a soft centre of spiritual vulnerability; there was McCartney, laying bare his romantic hopes and needs on the likes of 'The Night Before', 'Another Girl' and 'I've Just Seen

Above: (L–R) Paul McCartney, John Lennon and George Harrison poolside at Cliveden House in Maidenhead during the making of *Help!*.

Opposite above & below: The Beatles find two different ways of getting about in the snow in Obertauern, Austria.

a Face'. George, too, was experimenting ever more expressively with the moon-in-June format on the winningly open-faced 'I Need You' and 'You Like Me Too Much'.

"This is, of course, also the album that included the perfect 'Yesterday', the McCartney composition often voted the best pop song of all time, and one that wasn't even a British single until a decade later. Less famously, it also contained another love letter with an honesty that was as uncompromising as it was unfashionable at the time: John's utterly charming 'It's Only Love', with its almost pleading candour. 'Is it right that you and I should fight, every night?' he sang. 'Why do I feel the way I do?'

"More widely lauded long players would follow, and soon: it was just four months later that the intrepid pacesetters would release *Rubber Soul,*

elevating themselves to yet another echelon of imagination. But as the staging post between the naivety of Beatlemania and the worldly innovation of later years, *Help!* is as beguiling now as it was in that summer of 1965."

Tom Robinson

"*Help!* was a more disappointing movie with not quite such good songs. I sometimes sing 'You've Got to Hide Your Love Away' live because of its relevance to the gay liberation movement and because it was written around the time of John Lennon's famous holiday in Spain with Brian Epstein. Whatever went on there, you can almost certainly detect John writing about Epstein saying, 'You've got to hide your love away.' I thought back then, 'That's almost how I feel'."

Above: Opening night of the Beatles 1965 European tour was June 20 at the Palais des Sports in France.

Opposite left: Paul McCartney "smokes" a giant cigarette while wearing a chewing gum wrapper.

Opposite right: Ringo Starr strikes an unusual pose with a guitar, a tin of cough sweets and a selection of flight bags.

What the Critics Said

"It's a gay infectious romp which doesn't let up in pace or sparkle from start to finish. The album maintains the Beatles' usual high standard and although (apart from 'Yesterday') it's largely the same mixture as before, it's a mixture renowned for its tonic properties."

Derek Johnson, *NME*

"Inconceivably [the Beatles] have written a whole new crop of unique, memorable songs performed with the Beatles' painless soul. They don't sound as if it hurts to sing with feeling."

Chris Welch, *Melody Maker*

"The movie is wonderful. Some of the songs are among the best John and Paul have written."

Film review, *Melody Maker*

Melody Maker polled Beatles fans about the film and the music in July 1965, asking the question, "Is the music up to standard?" Four fans' answers were featured: "Well up to standard"; "Only a few tunes are up to standard"; "It's the best music ever written"; "Easily the best music the Beatles have done".

"The Beatles' second movie was a light-swinging London goof but the real action is on the soundtrack. It was a fond farewell to the mop-top sweetness, paving the way for the groundbreaking experimentation of *Rubber Soul*. The album peaks higher than *A Hard Day's Night*, with some of the Beatles' most mind-bogglingly great songs."

Rolling Stone magazine

Above: Ringo Starr in his usual place at the drums.

Opposite: Perhaps Paul McCartney wonders if there are more questions than answers.

1965
Rubber Soul

This is the record that inspired Beach Boy Brian Wilson to create his 1966 masterpiece: "In December of 1966 I heard the album *Rubber Soul* by the Beatles. It was definitely a challenge to me. I immediately went to work on the songs for *Pet Sounds*."

Rubber Soul had begun life in October 1965 when the Beatles returned to the studio after nearly four months away. After finishing work on *Help!* the group had set off on a major tour of Europe in June and July. This was followed by a 10-city trek around America, which included meeting Elvis Presley in California and appearing on *The Ed Sullivan Show*.

After taking some time off in September the Beatles reassembled with George Martin and Norman Smith to record 'Run For Your Life' and a track entitled 'This Bird Has Flown'. Six more sessions took place in October, including a reworking of 'This Bird Has Flown', now called 'Norwegian Wood'. By November 11 the band had completed their sixth album, recording both 'You Won't See Me' and 'Girl' in just two takes in an all-night session lasting over 12 hours.

Two weeks before they finished their work in the studio, the Beatles visited Buckingham Palace to collect their MBE (Member of the British Empire) medals from the Queen. In December they set off on what would be their final UK tour, where they performed both 'Nowhere Man' and 'If I Needed Someone' from their new album.

Once again, the cover photograph for their new album was taken by Robert Freeman, who seemingly created the psychedelic, "stretched" image of the band by accident after shooting it in the garden of Lennon's house. The rounded, globule-style lettering was created by Charles Font and, according to the *Guardian* newspaper, became "a staple of poster art for the flower power generation".

The title *Rubber Soul* apparently came from McCartney as a play on the idea of white people singing soul music. It was the first album to be released by the Beatles without their name on the front cover, which was seen as a reflection of their success and the resulting impact they had on how their music was presented.

In the first week of its release *Rubber Soul* raced to the top of the UK album chart, displacing *The Sound of Music*, and stayed at number one for nine weeks until the soundtrack album took over once again.

Rubber Soul

Released December 3, 1965 (Parlophone)

Drive My Car
Norwegian Wood
    (This Bird Has Flown)
You Won't See Me
Nowhere Man
Think For Yourself
The Word
Michelle
What Goes On
Girl
I'm Looking Through You
In My Life
Wait
If I Needed Someone
Run For Your Life

Reached #1 in the UK, Australia, Germany and Sweden and #5 in France. It was placed at #5 on *Rolling Stone*'s 500 Greatest Albums of All Time.

Previous pages: The Beatles performing the single 'Day Tripper' at Twickenham Film Studios for their 1965 promo film.

Left: Paul McCartney (left) and John Lennon share musical ideas in Abbey Road Studios.

Opposite: (L–R) John Lennon, George Harrison, Ringo Starr and Paul McCartney at the bar having a pint during the filming of *Help!*.

Graham Gouldman

"The next album that really hit me was *Rubber Soul* in 1965 – that was a big game changer. There were no covers and from then on it was just phenomenal – you wondered where all this stuff was coming from. Brilliant songs, great lyrics … I think 'Norwegian Wood' is one of the greatest songs ever written.

"The beauty of the Beatles was that they opened the way lyrically for songwriters. No one compares to them and I do not like hearing Beatles covers – even though 10cc did do a version of 'Across the Universe'.

"The songs on *Rubber Soul* were informed by real events and it doesn't matter whether you know what a song means, you know you are in the presence of something great. A lot of Lennon's songs are obviously Dylan-influenced and he's not a bad person to be influenced by – he was the master."

Ray Connolly

"This is my favourite because of 'In My Life', 'Nowhere Man' and 'Girl' – these I sing to myself all the time. I just think it's almost folk music. It's just perfect. There is a Dylan influence and this album has some of John's best songs. When you listen to all 14 tracks you realise just how clever they were as songwriters, and in the midst of all this they put out 'Day Tripper' and 'We Can Work It Out' as a single.

"'Nowhere Man' was John trying to image himself as the ordinary bloke in the street. He seemed to be in a weird situation; he was unhappy with most things in his life – he was unhappy at home, he was unhappy at being a Beatle and he was unhappy with his weight. It was so reflective of the times.

"I asked a Jewish friend of mine if 'Girl' sounded like a middle-European Jewish song and he said that he knew what I meant with its melody. It has a ring of an old Middle Eastern folk song with an extraordinary vocal by John.

"'In My Life' is probably John's best song ever. His uncle was dead, his mum was dead and other people he knew had gone – it's a very personal song. It summed up the whole of John Lennon and his life at that time.

"*Rubber Soul* for me is John at his best – there are three of John's greatest songs, and Paul's songs were not as strong on this album – they were stronger on the next one. You could see where they were all going and developing as songwriters. They were all three-minute songs that weren't over-laden, I prefer this to any other album.

"I was quite impressed with the cover but didn't realise it was the first one without their name on it – which they didn't really need by then. I remember thinking at the time, 'Is it going to be a really druggy album?' and it wasn't. They were nearly all good popular songs. For me it is the best from the sixties alongside *Pet Sounds*."

Per Gessle

"I love the sleeve because I love John Lennon's jacket – I have the cover picture by Robert Freeman in my office in my studio. For me when I think about this album, I think about the sleeve and it's also a very cool title.

"'Norwegian Wood' is one of my favourite tracks, then 'Think For Yourself' with the fuzz guitar and 'Girl' because of that magic Lennon voice. There were three writers but there were also three singers, which meant you never got bored with their sound.

"Maybe the reason they were able to do all their music in such a short time was because there were three generators – they had so much energy and so many ideas that maybe they just had to pour it out. We will never see that sort of output again in our lifetime.

"Pop music's essence is to reflect the era when it is born."

Tom Robinson

"For me the best album is *Rubber Soul*, which pulled it all back together after a few patchy ones. It's real classic, classy songwriting. To pull that lot out – 'Norwegian Wood' with its sitar, 'Girl' with the sighs. All the songs sound as if they came from one album – every one of those songs had a trademark sound that came from those sessions and from those days.

"The cover picture of their elongated heads in front of what looked like a Christmas tree made it

Previous pages: The four Beatles take questions from the press after collecting their MBEs from Queen Elizabeth II in October 1965.

Opposite: The Beatles and actress Eleanor Bron share a box on the set of *Help!*.

Left: The Beatles enjoy a bike ride in the Bahamas.

the perfect present for their fans. Their faces were so famous they didn't have to put their name on the cover.

"Track by track the musical genres just switch the whole time – every one is different. It was a Beatles album and not an album of any particular musical genre. It's still got the great vocal harmonies, it's still like a four-piece band that knows how to play and sing together."

Johnnie Walker

"I loved both the albums to do with the films *A Hard Day's Night* and *Help!*, but *Rubber Soul* stands out for me. The amazing thing about that was that they were all their own songs including George Harrison. They were expressing themselves.

"I had just joined pirate radio in May 1966 so it was still a fresh album to play on the radio. It contained some of my favourite songs: 'I'm Looking Through You' was always a big favourite, 'You Won't See Me' is another big favourite and I remember on Radio Caroline playing 'Nowhere Man' for Prime Minister Harold Wilson, who was trying to close the pirate stations.

"Mostly you play singles on pirate radio but I remember playing 'Nowhere Man' and 'You Won't See Me' a lot – basically our Caroline format was one in (the Caroline Top 40) and one out (which could be anything). There was no single on the album and I think that at the time it was thought that if you put singles on the album, the fans would feel cheated.

"When you first got a new Beatles single you thought, 'Hang on, where are they going with this?' and then you'd play it a lot and the more you played it the more you grew to love it. It was always a test to keep up with what they were doing on each new record.

"Whenever they went into the studio it was the one safe place for them, where they were protected from all the madness that was going on outside. My love for the Beatles does lean towards those early years."

Tim Rice

"I don't think there is a bad track on *Rubber Soul* although you could probably say that about a lot of their albums. If seems to me to be the halfway point between still writing fairly conventional songs in structure but writing very clever and advanced lyrics and tunes within that structure.

"Sometimes – as with 'The White Album' – they got either too simplistic or too complex compared with what they did on *Rubber Soul* when they seemed to have the balance between sophistication and great simplicity totally mixed – and brilliantly.

"In a way they were still making two-and-a-half minute pop songs but they were really advanced songs even if the Beatles didn't release a single from the album. 'You Won't See Me' is one of my all-time favourites and 'Nowhere Man' was just wonderful, and when I first heard 'Drive My Car' I thought of 'Baby Let's Play House' by Elvis.

"'Michelle' is a great, great pop song and you could see it heading into Johnny Mathis territory as soon as it was released, and I think the schoolboy French adds to the charm of the song.

"This is the sixth album in three years, which is amazing, absolutely extraordinary. And they also came out with the single 'Day Tripper' and 'We Can Work It Out', which were brilliant and weren't even on the album which was quite staggering. In fact there is very little dross on the first six albums they released and by the time they got to *Rubber Soul* you did kind of expect it to be brilliant."

Above: (L–R) Paul McCartney, John Lennon and George Harrison share the spotlight during a concert.

Opposite: The Beatles pose for more portraits. Clockwise L–R: Paul McCartney, George Harrison, John Lennon and Ringo Starr

- George Martin (*Abbey Road*): "Around this time (1965) it's probably correct to say that I was as interested as they were in creating new sounds and experimenting in the studios. They were never the sort of people you put in a studio to make three-minute pop songs with a nice arrangement; they needed much more than that and that was the real joy of working with them."

- George Martin (*The Complete Beatles Recording Sessions*): "It was the first album to present a new, growing Beatles to the world. For the first time we began to think of albums as art on their own, as complete entities."

- Geoff Emerick (*Here, There and Everywhere*): "Though everyone agreed that it had quite a few good songs and a crisp, clean sound, the general feeling among the staff that were working on it was that it was a pleasant diversion into the realm of folk and country music. But this was just idle chatter around the canteen table."

- Pete Brown (*The Love You Make*): "*Rubber Soul* was something of a critical disappointment. Although it was in the Top Ten album charts for over seven months – four of them in the Number One position – it was a puzzlement to the confused kids expecting to hear more juvenile 'yeah, yeah, yeah' songs. It was the best of the many challenges the Beatles posed to their fans: to keep up."

- Graham Coxon (*Liverpool Echo*): "I always say *Rubber Soul* is my favourite Beatles album. I like the way it's recorded – you can hear microphone feedback, there are no effects and it sounds great. The most influential thing about all the Beatles songs for me was that anything more or anything less would ruin them."

Opposite: Paul McCartney in Abbey Road Studio 2, complete with seaweed-filled sound proofing.

Above: Paul McCartney finds time to put his feet up in the studio control room.

What the Beatles Said

"We were getting better technically and musically. We finally took over the studio. I think *Rubber Soul* was about when it started happening. *Rubber Soul* was a matter of having all experienced the recording studio; having grown musically as well but [having] the knowledge of the place, of the studio. We were more precise about making the album, that's all, and we took over the cover and everything. *Rubber Soul* was the pot album and *Revolver* was the acid."

John Lennon (*The Beatles Anthology*)

Opposite: Ringo Starr's Churchillian impression outside 10 Downing Street.

Below: The Beatles in rehearsal for the *Blackpool Night Out* TV show in August 1965.

"George Martin was very understanding, even though we were going to change style and get more psychedelic or surreal. It never seemed to throw him even though sometimes it was not quite his taste in music."

Paul McCartney (*The Beatles Anthology*)

"There was a lot of experimentation on *Rubber Soul*, influenced, I think, by the substances."

Ringo Starr (*The Beatles Anthology*)

"*Rubber Soul* was my favourite album, even at that time. I think it was the best one we made; we certainly knew we were making a good album. But the most important thing about it was that we were suddenly hearing sounds that we weren't able to hear before.

"I liked the way we got our faces to be longer on the album cover. We lost the 'little innocents' tag, the naivety, and *Rubber Soul* was the first one where we were fully fledged potheads."

George Harrison (*The Beatles Anthology*)

"Finally we took over the studio. We were learning the technique on *Rubber Soul*. We were more precise about the album, that's all, and we took over the cover and everything.

John Lennon (*The Beatles: In Their Own Words*)

Left, above: Paul McCartney collects an Ivor Novello Award on behalf of the Beatles in 1965.

Left: John Lennon stands for the camera on the set of *Help!*.

Opposite: Who's looking at who? (L–R) George Harrison, Paul McCartney, Ringo Starr and John Lennon framed on the set of *Help!*.

What the Critics Said

"[The] great thing about this LP is that the Beatles are still finding different ways to make us enjoy listening to their music. Altogether a good album."

Allen Evans, *NME*

"The Beatles' new 14-track album is not their best on first hearing. Without a shadow of a doubt, the Beatles' sound has matured – but unfortunately it also seems to have become a little subdued. Several of the tracks almost become monotonous, an unBeatles feature if ever there was one. A record certainly worthy of a place in your collection but maybe it's just that we expect too much from the Beatles!"

Pop Panel review, *Melody Maker*

"One marvels and wonders at the constant stream of melodic ingenuity from the boys, both as performers and composers. Keeping up their pace of creativeness is quite fantastic."

Album review, *Record Mirror*

"If recorded by anyone else but the Beatles, [it] would not be worthy of release."

Richard Green, *Record Mirror*

"The biggest indignity in Beatledom ... is that *Rubber Soul* is so often overlooked. It contained no hits, yet would be the highlight of a lesser band's discography."

1001 Albums You Must Hear Before You Die

Left: (L–R) George Harrison, manager Brian Epstein and Ringo Starr on their way to Manila, the Philippines, in July 1966.

Overleaf: Frenzied Beatles fans scream for their heroes.

1966
Revolver

Revolver

Released August 5, 1966
(Parlophone)

Taxman
Eleanor Rigby
I'm Only Sleeping
Love You To
Here, There And Everywhere
Yellow Submarine
She Said She Said
Good Day Sunshine
And Your Bird Can Sing
For No One
Doctor Robert
I Want To Tell You
Got To Get You Into My Life
Tomorrow Never Knows

Reached #1 in the UK,
Australia, Germany and
Sweden, #5 in France.
The album was voted
#3 in *Rolling Stone*
magazine's 500 Greatest
Albums of All Time.

Following the release of *Rubber Soul* in time for Christmas 1965, the Beatles took a long overdue break during the first three months of 1966. John, Paul and Ringo relaxed on holiday while George Harrison got married to actress and model Patti Boyd and went off on honeymoon.

They all returned to the studio in the first week of April to begin work on their seventh UK album and immediately started work on a song tentatively titled 'Mark 1', which would eventually become the final track on the new album under the name 'Tomorrow Never Knows'.

The four Beatles worked continuously for nearly a fortnight on the 14 tracks that, for the first time, included three songs by Harrison. In the middle of these sessions they took time out from making the album to record the number one single 'Paperback Writer' – their 10th consecutive UK chart topper – and then completed their 11th hit single 'Eleanor Rigby' over two days at the end of April.

A further week of recording in May was followed by another seven days in June with the final two tracks – 'Here There and Everywhere' and 'Got to Get You Into My Life' – being completed on June 17.

With the album finished, the Beatles set off on a tour of Germany, which was followed by concerts

Previous pages: (L–R) John Lennon, Ringo Starr, Paul McCartney and George Harrison collect their 1966 *NME* awards from American film and TV star Clint Walker.

Above: George Harrison and Patti Boyd, who married in January 1966.

Opposite: John Lennon arrives at London Airport from the Philippines in July 1966.

in the Philippines and Japan before they visited America in August for what would turn out to be their last ever concert tour. The band had already performed for the final time in Britain at the NME Poll Winners Concert on May 1.

Revolver was not the first choice of title for the new album. *Abracadabra, Magic Circle, Four Sides to the Circle* and even *Bubble and Squeak* were some of the suggestions before they settled on *Revolver* – a reference to the movement of a record turntable rather than a handgun.

After working on five Beatles album covers Robert Freeman was relegated to the back of the sleeve as the group turned to artist and musician Klaus Voorman to create a psychedelic montage of his drawings and photographs of them.

Berlin-born Voorman had actually seen the Beatles play live during their time in Hamburg in 1960 and had dated Astrid Kirchherr before she met their one-time bassist Stuart Sutcliffe. When Voorman moved to Britain he met the musicians Paddy Chambers and Gibson Kemp, who became Paddy, Klaus & Gibson and were briefly managed by Brian Epstein before breaking up.

Voorman then replaced Jack Bruce as the bass player in Manfred Mann and played on a host of hit records while still designing and drawing. As the Beatles worked on their new album, John Lennon invited Voorman to design the artwork for their next release. "John called me and asked if I had any ideas that I might want to use for the cover," he says. "I did a few rough sketches and went to them with scribbles."

Those "scribbles" won him a Grammy award in 1966 for Best Album Cover, Graphic Arts for *Revolver*. Voorman later played on solo releases by Lennon, Starr and Harrison and also worked with Carly Simon and Harry Nilsson.

Revolver entered the UK album chart at Number One, replacing *The Sound of Music* (again!), and held the top spot for seven weeks before being replaced by ... *The Sound of Music*. Since they first topped the UK album chart in April 1963, the Beatles' seven studio albums had held the Number One position for a total of 108 weeks and spent a grand total of 318 weeks in the chart.

Left: After an absence of over three years, the Beatles returned to Germany for a show at Munich's Circus-Krone-Bau in June 1966.

Chris Thomas

"When *Revolver* came out there just seemed to be so many innovative things on it. I just found that *Revolver* changed the course of everything. I thought *Sgt. Pepper* was a manifestation of the stuff that had been done on *Revolver*, which has the real groundbreaking stuff on it.

"Starting off with Paul's guitar solo on 'Taxman' – which was so odd you went, 'What's that?' And then there's 'Tomorrow Never Knows', which I think sounded weird to a listener but it's different if you are actually making a record; you have a different view of stuff.

"To my ears a lot of this was stuff I hadn't heard before and I couldn't really work out the references, which again is amazing – to be able to create something without the listener being able to discover the references. It was just groundbreaking.

"I loved it and every single song is fantastic. The songwriting was perfect. 'Here, There and Everywhere' is just one of the best songs Paul has ever written. To me it's just an amazing album; even 'Yellow Submarine' was cleverly done: it was a laugh but it's not a throwaway. There's not a dud on the record, which is an incredible achievement.

"The image that comes into my mind is that it's stark in the sense that there's no huge amount of production stuff in there. *Sgt. Pepper* was in technicolor and this is in black and white and the cover really illustrates what the record was about. *Revolver* was such an efficient record, there's no evidence really of much overdubbing, it's chiselled down to the bare bones."

Ken Townsend

"I think the most significant for me would be *Revolver* as it was the first one on which we used a lot of ADT [artificial double-tracking], which I invented. I was called in by the studio manager Chick Fowler, who said, 'Here Ken, you get on all right with the Beatles don't you?' I did get on with them pretty well – if they called people by their surnames it wasn't very good but if they used your first names you were all right. I was called Ken.

"So I was thrown into the *Revolver* sessions in April 1966 to help Geoff Emerick, who was promoted to engineer to replace Norman Smith. I was told by Fowler to sit behind him to make sure he got on all right – he actually did very well even though the Beatles were a bit apprehensive.

"They wanted to move on and experiment with sounds. John and Paul came up with ideas of what they wanted and you had to think of how you could do them. They wanted something different and having four-track and ADT meant we could do new things.

"Later the sessions were getting more interesting. I was a design engineer who trained at Hayes and liked to be tested to do things differently. I found it all quite intriguing and it was a lot more interesting than just coming in and recording a straight song."

Per Gessle

"I always say 1966 is the best year for pop music – and that's because of *Revolver*, which is such a great album. 'And Your Bird Can Sing' is my favourite track and 'Taxman' is such a great song. 'Here, There and Everywhere' was played at my wedding; and they make it sound simple but if you try to play it, it's really complicated.

Above: Americans set fire to Beatles albums in protest at John Lennon's "more popular then Jesus" remark.

Opposite: John Lennon faces the press after the Beatles returned from concerts in Manila.

"It is almost perfect and I love the album sleeve by Klaus Voorman. It is much heavier than *Rubber Soul*. It's the last album where the songs were classic Beatles pop music but still had that edge in the production and the sound.

"The guitar sound is heavier, it has much more rock to it than *Rubber Soul*, which is much more of a pop record; and I think that's what appeals to musicians and writers about *Revolver* – the hardest thing to do as a writer is to come up with a great pop song and make it raw, make it rough.

"In 1981 before Roxettte I had a band called Gyllene Tider and we were the biggest band [in Sweden] at that time. We did release a special EP with four cover versions including the Beatles 'And Your Bird Can Sing', which I translated into Swedish – and it sounds really terrible. We tried to make it similar but weren't capable. We were in our early twenties and it was just like a throwaway thing – you could do that back then, just after punk and new wave – but today you can't really touch that stuff.

Tom Robinson

"I was 16 and saved up my pocket money and bought my copy of *Revolver* and I listened to it many, many times over and I was deeply disappointed. I think that it was "The White Album" [*The Beatles*] early. It was them fragmenting and going their own sweet way and indulging themselves. I don't rate it and personally I think that's because they'd become mega-famous, the ball kept rolling and it all snowballed."

Johnnie Walker

"If I'm going for a second album I would go for *Revolver*, which was a groundbreaking album and the one that prepared the way for *Sgt. Pepper*.

"They were coming up to their last ever gig in San Francisco and were really moving into becoming a studio band – they could do all these different things. George Martin was a very straight guy who always looked so conventional in his shirt and tie, but was willing to help them to break all the rules of studio recording and help them with experimenting.

Right: The Beatles played their final European concert at Hamburg Ernst Merck Halle in June 1966.

"'Tomorrow Never Knows' really gives you an idea of what might happen in the future and who knew what 'I'm Only Sleeping' was all about. 'Here, There and Everywhere' is an absolute masterpiece but not so much 'Yellow Submarine', which is the token Ringo lead vocal.

"There were two great songs that I called 'uppers': they were the feelgood songs 'Good Day Sunshine' and 'And Your Bird Can Sing', which follow each other (which I always thought wasn't particularly good running order placement). 'Eleanor Rigby' was wonderful and I've always been a friend of strings on record – it just sounds beautiful.

"With their great success came the freedom to be experimental. Other groups were under tremendous pressure to keep the same sort of sound and take the same approach because that was what their fans wanted; but the Beatles had enough success to really take a chance and step out on a limb. That became the impetus for artists such as Brian Wilson to push the boundaries as well."

Glen Matlock
"*Revolver*, that's probably my favourite Beatles album although it does have 'Yellow Submarine' on it. Their sound has developed but with better songs than on *Rubber Soul*."

Barbara Dickson
"I don't think *Revolver* is as self-indulgent as *Sgt. Pepper*. It's got real structure, which is why I like it, and it has that really great Indian influence of the time; it is very much of the time but it's just great. Its structure, it's got form, the songs are interesting and are not too poppy and lightweight."

Above: Paul McCartney goes for stripes.

Opposite: A portrait of Yoko Ono before her marriage to John Lennon.

Overleaf: (L–R) George Harrison, Ringo Starr, Paul McCartney and John Lennon caught on camera during their trip to Tokyo in 1966.

- Elvis Costello, in *Rolling Stone* magazine's 2004 edition celebrating the "100 Greatest Artists of All Time": "My absolute favourite albums are *Rubber Soul* and *Revolver*. When you picked up *Revolver*, you knew it was something different. Heck, they are wearing sunglasses indoors in the picture on the back of the cover and not even looking at the camera ... and the music was so strange and yet so vivid. If I had to pick a favourite song from those albums, it would be 'And Your Bird Can Sing' ... no, 'Girl' ... no, 'For No One' ... and so on, and so on ..."

- Liverpool-born Ian McNabb (*Liverpool Echo*): "All the Beatles albums have something to recommend them but my favourite is *Revolver*. The songs got more complicated and saw McCartney's stock rise massively.
  "Tape loops appeared for the first time on a pop record, Indian raga could be heard on a western pop record. This was all done on a four-track machine. In 1966. Three years after 'She Loves You'! It's absolutely mind-blowing. The world would never be the same."

- Noel Gallagher (interviewed on *Quietus*): "*Revolver* was when the sitars really started to come in with the Beatles and all the backwards stuff on 'Tomorrow Never Knows'. It's their first drug album. It's a cliché to talk about it now because it's so well known but this is a mind-blowing album. The psychedelic stuff they did after this was mind-blowing and the Fab Four mop top stuff before this was equally good but on this record it all came together."

- Liverpool-born Melanie 'Sporty Spice' Chisholm (*Liverpool Echo*): "*Revolver* is my favourite Beatles album. The whole city is still very, very proud of them. Growing up, you would hear the Beatles in pubs and shops the whole time. I like *Revolver* because it's an album of pop songs but they were experimenting with the old Indian vibe as well."

- Geoff Emerick (*Here, There and Everywhere*): "Incredibly, *Revolver* had been completed in just over ten weeks (we had most weekends off), with many songs taking only a few hours to get down on tape. It was always a matter of capturing the moment, and when you were working with the Beatles it had to be right. Exhausting as it was, both mentally and physically, it was a good way to work – really the *only* way to work."

- Pete Brown (*The Love You Make*): "*Revolver* closed with a harbinger of things to come. Other songs on the album had been influenced by LSD but John's 'Tomorrow Never Knows' is the first all-out acid trip."

- George Martin (*Abbey Road*): "The studio became a workshop, a permanent experimental thing. It seemed to work for [the band] and tracks became things that everybody got involved with. On something like 'Tomorrow Never Knows' it became a combination of tape loops ... with people – including the Beatles – holding the tape tension by mean of a pencil; and we had a total of eight machines in different control rooms throughout the studio, all linked up."

- George Martin (*All You Need Is Ears*): "'Eleanor Rigby' and 'Tomorrow Never Knows' had been strong hints, for those with ears to hear, at what was to come. They were forerunners of a complete change of style. I did realise that something was happening in the music and that excited me."

- Tony Barrow (*John, Paul, George, Ringo & Me*): "One redeeming feature of 1966 was the release of what I consider to be the Beatles best-ever album – *Revolver* – in the middle of a year that in many other ways would be best forgotten. My strongest memory of the visit to Germany (in 1966) is not of the concerts or the reunions but of hearing my favourite Beatles album for the first time and helping to come up with a title for it.

  "Sitting in a circle with the four boys, I first heard the completed album on George's tape recorder in the Munich hotel and immediately decided that this was the Fab Four's most attractive collection to date.

  "As for finding an album title to fit ... we went round in circles from *Magic Circle* and *Four Sides To The Circle* to Paul's suggestion *Pendulum* and Ringo's frivolous one, *After Geography*, his cryptic nod to the Stones' *Aftermath*, before the group agreed unanimously to call it *Revolver*."

Left: The Beatles face the Japanese media in Tokyo.

Opposite: George Harrison and John Lennon in harmony during the Beatles' final German concert.

Exhale Wellness A

Bud Pop
Cheef Botanecal
Hollweed CBD
Fab CBD

naturalstacks.com
serutonan

Performance lab 4

Dopamine Brain Food
naturalstacks.com

What the Beatles Said

"We have used a few odd instruments but because they sound like they ought to be in the song. Some of them are unusual for us.

"Normally we go into the studios with, say, eight numbers of our own, some old numbers or some numbers we used to know which we do up a bit. This time we had all our own numbers – including three from George – so we've had to work them all out. I think it'll be our best album yet."

Paul McCartney (*Melody Maker*, June 1966)

"One thing's for sure: the next LP [*Revolver*] is going to be very different. We wanted to have it so that there was no space between the tracks – just continuous. But they wouldn't wear it."

John Lennon (*The Beatles Anthology*)

"*Revolver* has that quality of *Rubber Soul* because it's the follow-on. We were really starting to find ourselves in the studio. We were finding what we could do, just being the four of us and playing our instruments. The songs got more interesting so with that the effects got more interesting. I think the drugs were kicking in a little more heavily on this album."

Ringo Starr (*The Beatles Anthology*)

"For the *Revolver* sleeve we moved away from Robert Freeman to Klaus Vormann. Klaus was a good artist and a really good friend of ours. He did a good job and it became quite a classic album cover.

"*Revolver* was accepted well. I don't see much difference between *Rubber Soul* and *Revolver*. To me, they could be Volume One and Volume Two."

George Harrison (*The Beatles Anthology*)

Below: John Lennon with actor Roy Kinnear (left) in the film *How I Won the War*.

Opposite above: The Beatles play their final UK concert at the 1966 NME Poll Winners show.

Opposite below: German Beatles fans came out in their thousands for the group's concerts in 1966.

The Beatles began working on *Sgt. Pepper* **in November 1966 after five months away from the studio, during which time they played their final live concert – in San Francisco's Candlestick Park on August 29.**

When they started recording 'Strawberry Fields', Lennon, McCartney, Harrison and Starr assumed it would be included on the album. But when it was coupled with 'Penny Lane' and issued as a single in February 1967, the band moved on and focused on a collection that would not include these two hit songs.

In early December 1966, just days before the December 9 release of their first compilation album, *A Collection of Beatles Oldies*, the group began work

on 'When I'm Sixty-Four'. From then on they eagerly embraced their new-found freedom as a "studio band", without the distractions of live shows or TV appearances, and continued over the next four months to complete a further 12 tracks. George Harrison's 'Within You Without You', recorded on April 3, was the final piece in the jigsaw.

Midway through the recording of *Sgt. Pepper* the Beatles set aside an evening to record a 24-bar orchestral piece, with a 40-piece orchestra, to fill a gap in the song 'A Day in the Life'. During the five-hour session on February 10, the orchestra, the Beatles plus assorted friends such as Mick Jagger, Keith Richards, Marianne Faithfull, Donovan and Mike Nesmith gathered in Abbey Road's Studio 1.

At the Beatles' request some members of the orchestra, dressed in dinner jackets, also donned clowns' noses, silly hats and fake bald heads. The whole session was filmed for a proposed TV

Sgt. Pepper's Lonely Hearts Club Band

Released June 1, 1967 (Parlophone)

Sgt. Pepper's Lonely Hearts Club Band

With a Little Help from My Friends

Lucy in the Sky with Diamonds

Getting Better

Fixing a Hole

She's Leaving Home

Being for the Benefit of Mr. Kite!

Within You Without You

When I'm Sixty-Four

Lovely Rita

Good Morning Good Morning

Sgt. Pepper's Lonely Hearts Club Band (Reprise)

A Day in the Life

Reached #1 in the UK, the USA, Australia, Canada, Germany, Norway and Sweden. The album was listed #1 in *Rolling Stone*'s 500 Greatest Albums of All Time and in the *NME*'s 100 All Time Best Albums (1974). The UK's Official Charts Company places it at #3 on the list of biggest-selling UK albums of all time (behind compilation collections by Queen and Abba), with sales of 5.1 million. It is the bestselling British studio album in pop history.

Previous pages: (L–R) Ringo Starr, Maureen Starr, Jane Asher, Paul McCartney, George Harrison, Patti Harrison, Cynthia Lennon and John Lennon sitting in front of the Maharishi Mahesh Yogi in India.

Left: Paul McCartney and John Lennon at work on the *Sgt. Pepper* album.

Opposite: The hand-painted caravan John Lennon bought as a present for his son Julian.

special on the making of *Sgt. Pepper*, which was never completed.

Four years after completing their debut album in just a day at a cost of around £400, the Beatles spent four months in the studio making *Sgt. Pepper* at a record cost of over £25,000. Having created their most ambitious album to date they needed a cover design to go with it.

The idea of creating an alternative group – Sgt. Pepper's band – was Paul McCartney's; and it was left to the artists Peter Blake and his then wife Jann Haworth to come up with a suitably revolutionary sleeve design. It was Blake who devised the idea of having a crowd standing behind the "band", and he invited the Beatles to come up with the names of people they wanted to appear on the cover.

The final total of 57 photographs was used together with eight waxworks, including those of the four Beatles, borrowed from Madame

Above: John Lennon and Paul McCartney busy making music for the *Magical Mystery Tour* record.

Left: John Lennon on board the *Magical Mystery Tour* bus.

Opposite: The Beatles at the launch of their *Sgt. Pepper* album at manager Brian Epstein's London home.

Tussauds. They featured film stars, sportsmen, musicians, artists, writers, scientists and politicians. As it turned out, they were not all chosen by the Beatles: Blake was forced to substitute John Lennon's choices of Jesus, Gandhi and Adolf Hitler, all vetoed by EMI.

The cost of the final gatefold cover artwork, which was photographed by Michael Cooper, has been estimated at around £3,000 – at a time when most covers cost £100. On the day of its release, complete with printed lyrics and a set of cut-outs, it was promoted as "the most expensive packaging of any pop album ever".

When *Sgt. Pepper's Lonely Hearts Club Band* was released on June 1 it became the first and only Beatles album to be issued on a Thursday, not the UK's traditional Friday. It was also the first Beatles album to be released simultaneously around the world with the same tracklisting and artwork.

With first-week sales of over 250,000, the album entered the British album chart at Number One, displacing *The Sound of Music*, and stayed there for 23 weeks. *Sgt. Pepper* was replaced eventually by the same soundtrack but returned to top the chart on three more occasions – twice for one week and once for two weeks – notching up a total of 28 weeks as the UK's bestselling album. All in all it spent a record-breaking 148 weeks on the chart.

In America the first "global" Beatles album hit the Number One spot and held it for 15 weeks. The following February the Beatles and George Martin collected Grammy Awards for Album of the Year; and artists Peter Blake and Jann Haworth and engineer Geoff Emerick also won awards for Best Album Cover, Graphic Arts and Best Engineered Recording, respectively.

Bizarrely, it would be another 10 years before *Sgt. Pepper* was officially recognized by the British music industry. At the inaugural 1977 BRIT Awards (then called the British Record Industry Britannia Centenary Awards, celebrating the 100th anniversary of recorded sound), *Sgt. Pepper* was voted Best British Album and the Beatles were named Best British Pop Group.

Right: Paul McCartney conducts the 40-piece orchestra during 'A Day In The Life' sessions in Abbey Road Studios.

Bart van Poppel

"It was 1967, I was 11 years old and standing in line at the local record store trying to obtain a copy of the latest Beatles LP, *Sgt. Pepper's Lonely Hearts Club Band*. Initially I intended to buy it as a present for my parents, but after I played it for the first time in my room it stayed there forever.

"I was completely knocked down by the incredible sounds I heard: the beautiful songs, the diversity of styles and its brilliant production. Not just guitars, keyboards and drums, but accompanied with strings, brass, woodwinds, all sorts of exotic organs and even Indian traditional instruments. And let's not forget the groundbreaking cover by Peter Blake, which I studied for hours and hours. Me, my friends and lots of other Beatle fans were completely surprised by this sensational album.

"And now, more than 50 years later I am a member of a band called the Analogues and we play 'live' from start to finish the Beatles albums they never performed themselves. They stopped playing live in 1966 just after the release of *Revolver*, the first of six fantastic albums on which the Beatles used all possible facilities of the recording studio.

"In 2017 it was *Sgt. Pepper*'s 50th birthday, so time for the Analogues to perform my favourite Beatles album. I don't know how many times I put the LP on my record player in those 50 years; I had every single note in my head, but now I had to listen to *Pepper* in a different way.

"We had to analyze the material and think of how to play these great and complex songs for a 'live' audience in the flow of the album. The first five songs are not the most difficult ones. We got 'Sgt. Pepper' (the overture) with four French horn

Opposite: The Beatles' Apple boutique in London, which stayed open for just eight months.

Below: Paul McCartney and George Harrison and their partners make their way to the premiere of *How I Won the War*.

overdubbed and mixed to sound like more and I think it was possibly the first time musicians played back to a track which came through speakers into the studio as we didn't have earphones.

"The speakers were behind George Martin on the podium and facing us so we could hear the music the Beatles had recorded. We played on top of the bits of Beatles music that involved us – not the whole song. We did takes with us playing over the Beatles music and also did it a few times separately.

"Paul McCartney, who did some conducting, came round the orchestra and in my case he explained the glissando from low to high, crescendoing, while George Martin was conducting. As we were only doing a musical sweep-up – there was no rhythm at all – very little proper conducting was needed. But I do think I was

the first session percussionist to play on a Beatles recording as they usually did all the percussion stuff themselves.

"The Beatles were all there, watching and listening in the control room with their then girlfriends or wives. Of course we – as mainly classical session players – didn't really know them at that point. They were famous but not the icons we now know them to be.

"I heard tracks from *Sgt. Pepper* on the radio and through friends and didn't have a copy until it came out on CD; but I still didn't realize anything about the track I was on. I didn't know I was on it so there wasn't an incentive to buy it.

"Back then, classical and pop music were two different worlds, unlike now when they all cross over. I was into classical music and more aware of

Previous pages: The Beatles proudly show off their latest album at the May 1967 launch of *Sgt. Pepper*.

Left: Paul McCartney lays down another bass line during an Abbey Road session.

Overleaf: Happy days for Ringo Starr and George Harrison as they promote their 'All You Need Is Love' TV broadcast.

Sgt. Pepper's Lonely Hearts Club Band

- Geoff Emerick (*Here, There and Everywhere*): "Another hallmark of *Sgt. Pepper* was that the Beatles were starting to get fed up with using the same instrumentation all the time. They wanted to advance themselves and were becoming increasingly frustrated with the same old two-guitar, bass-and-drums line-up.

  "With *Sgt. Pepper*, everything came together. The Beatles were looking to go out on a limb, both musically and sonically, and I was willing to climb out there with them. Somehow it all worked."

- Peter Asher (interviewed by the author): "My ambition to become a producer was inspired by *Sgt. Pepper*. Every time you hear a really good record, as a producer, you wonder how they did that. That was the case with *Sgt. Pepper*. It was a period of great experimentation."

- Pete Brown (*The Love You Make*): "The twelve songs on *Sgt. Pepper* set a new standard of achievement in popular music. *Sgt. Pepper* became not only the album of the summer but the album that most perfectly personified the incense-laden, rainbow coloured, psychedelic sixties themselves. It functioned as an anthem, orchestrating our lives."

- George Martin (*Abbey Road*): "Technically, *Sgt. Pepper* was not particularly innovative. I've heard it described as a watershed but I don't agree."

- George Martin (*All You Need Is Ears*): "A lot of the sounds on records like *Sgt. Pepper* are made by legitimate instruments, but the use of them doesn't necessarily correspond to what you would hear in a concert hall. On the *Sgt. Pepper* album we did all sorts of things with the stereo effect. We had things in absurd positions."

  "For my part I felt it was the album which turned the Beatles from being an ordinary rock 'n' roll group into being significant contributors to the history of artistic performance. It was a turning point – *the* turning point."

- Howard Goodall (*Daily Express*): "It's almost impossible to pick one Beatles album but their musical imaginations reached a peak of inventiveness and colour with *Sgt. Pepper*, probably the most influential pop record in history. Magical, witty, disarming, unexpected, bounteously tuneful, charmingly kaleidoscopic, unapologetically English and bursting with energy, youth and a sense of discovery."

What the Beatles Said

"*Sgt. Pepper* is the one. It was a peak."

"*Sgt. Pepper* is one of the most important steps in our career. It had to be just right."
John Lennon (*The Beatles: In Their Own Words*)

"*Sgt. Pepper* was our grandest endeavour. It gave everybody – including me – a lot of leeway to come up with ideas and to try different material."
Ringo Starr (*The Beatles Anthology*)

"How can we tour when we are making stuff like we're doing on the new album?"

"When you get down to it, it was nothing more than an album called *Sgt. Pepper* with the tracks stuck together. It was a beautiful idea then but it doesn't mean a thing now."
John Lennon (*The Beatles Anthology*)

"After the record was finished I thought it was great. I thought it was a huge advance. "Everyone said 'Ah! A *concept* album!' It was the first time I'd heard the word. The mood of the album was the spirit of the age."
Paul McCartney (*The Beatles Anthology*)

Opposite: John Lennon gets off the *Magical Mystery Tour* bus in Newquay.

Right: Paul McCartney and John Lennon enjoy some sea air on the beach in Cornwall.

With the album *Sgt. Pepper*, the singles 'All You Need Is Love' and 'Lady Madonna' and the EP 'Magical Mystery Tour' all behind them, the Beatles took time out during the spring of 1968 and travelled to India for a planned three-month stay at the Maharishi Mahesh Yogi's retreat.

John and Cynthia Lennon travelled with George Harrison and Pattie Boyd to the guru's ashram at Rishikesh in mid-February. They were joined four days later by Ringo and Maureen Starr, and Paul McCartney and his girlfriend Jane Asher. They were among 60 other people – including musicians Donovan and Mike Love and actress Mia Farrow – training to teach transcendental meditation. While Mr and Mrs Starr left after just 10 days, McCartney stayed for five weeks. The Lennons and the Harrisons didn't leave the Himalayan retreat till April 12.

Even though all the Beatles left earlier than planned, the visit to India proved to be a fruitful period in terms of songwriting. They spent much of their time creating the music that would eventually appear on their one and only studio double album.

Armed with a clutch of new songs, the Beatles returned to Abbey Road on May 30 to begin work, starting with Lennon's 'Revolution' (which would become 'Revolution 1'). Also in the studio that day, alongside producer George Martin and engineer Geoff Emerick, were Lennon's new girlfriend Yoko Ono and Martin's new assistant Chris Thomas.

Recording continued throughout June and July – when Emerick walked out on the group and the album – and into August, when there was a brief trip to Trident Studios in Soho to record 'Dear Prudence'. September saw the Beatles back in the familiar surroundings of Abbey Road; and this time

The Beatles

Released November 22, 1968 (Apple/Parlophone)

Back in the USSR

Dear Prudence

Glass Onion

Ob-La-Di, Ob-La-Da

Wild Honey Pie

The Continuing Story of Bungalow Bill

While My Guitar Gently Weeps

Happiness Is a Warm Gun

Martha My Dear

I'm So Tired

Blackbird

Piggies

Rocky Raccoon

Don't Pass Me By

Why Don't We Do It in the Road

I Will

Julia

Birthday

Yer Blues

Mother Nature's Son

Everybody's Got Something to Hide Except Me and My Monkey

Sexy Sadie

Helter Skelter

Long, Long, Long

Revolution 1

Honey Pie

Savoy Truffle

Cry Baby Cry

Revolution 9

Good Night

Reached #1 in the UK, Australia, Canada, France, Germany, Norway, Spain, Sweden and the USA. Voted #10 on *Rolling Stone's* 500 Greatest Albums of All Time and named by the same title as Album of the Year in 1968.

they were joined by Eric Clapton, who Harrison had recruited to play on his song, 'While My Guitar Gently Weeps'.

At the end of the first week of September, Martin went off on holiday, leaving Chris Thomas a note telling him to make himself "available to the Beatles". The result was that Thomas took over as producer for nearly three weeks until Martin returned to the band and to Trident to record four tracks during the first week of October.

After a further week in Abbey Road, the band finished the album on October 14 with the completion of 'Savoy Truffle'. Lennon and McCartney then worked out the running order and edited the master tape during an all-night session starting on October 16.

Sometime during the recording sessions, McCartney met the renowned pop artist Richard Hamilton and briefed him to design the artwork for the album. He began by creating a collage of photographs of the four Beatles, which would be used as a giveaway poster alongside four portraits taken by John Kelly. But when it came to actual sleeve design, Hamilton and McCartney settled on a plain white cover – as a complete contrast to the colourful *Sgt. Pepper* images.

It was then decided that the new album should be called simply *The Beatles*. The group's name would be embossed on the sleeve and each copy of the record would be given a serial number. The plain white cover led to the album being dubbed "The White Album"; and Hamilton's idea of

Previous pages: John Lennon and George Harrison relaxing on the banks of the River Ganges in India.

Above: (L–R) George Harrison joins actors Rita Tushingham and Michael York for a sitar session in EMI's studios in Bombay.

Opposite: (L–R) Yoko Ono, John Lennon and Paul McCartney in their seats for the premiere of Lennon's play *In His Own Write.*

"millions" of copies of numbered albums failed to materialize. McCartney once said, "I think EMI only did a few thousand and then gave up."

While Lennon claimed he got number 000001 – "because he shouted loudest" – this copy of the album was eventually sold by Starr at auction in America in 2015 for $790,000. Number 000005 fetched £19,000 in 2018.

The Beatles was released with advance orders of over one million, while EMI reported that they shipped 100,000 copies on the first day of sales. It was the group's first album to appear on the new Apple label – following the creation of Apple Corps in early 1968 – but as the group were still officially signed to EMI, The White Album appeared with a Parlophone catalogue number.

At the time of the album's release, there was talk that the Beatles would pay for, and appear in, TV commercials to promote the new record; but the estimated cost of around £16,000 was, according to NME, considered by somebody at Apple to be too great. A plan to paint half a dozen London buses white and write *The Beatles* on the sides was also abandoned.

When the group's 30-track double album was issued, it shot to Number One on December 7, 1968 and ended another album's record-breaking run. *The Sound of Music* had first topped the British chart in June 1965 and, over the next three years, held the Number One spot for a total of 70 weeks, deposing the Beatles five times. The Beatles' White Album displaced it for the last time, notching up eight consecutive weeks at the top and nine in the USA.

Opposite: John Lennon and Yoko Ono get a police escort after appearing at Marylebone Magistrate's Court in October 1968.

Above, left: News of John Lennon and Yoko Ono being arrested made the headlines.

Above: John Lennon and Yoko Ono at the Robert Fraser gallery in London where they launched 365 'You Are Here' balloons.

Diederik Nomden

"Simultaneously with trying to learn to play the guitar – it must have been in 1991 or 1992 – I got turned on to the Beatles' famous White Album. Of course, I knew the Beatles and most of their hits, but this was really something else. As I was just starting to play, I needed a few simple songs to hone my skills. The White Album came at exactly the right time.

"Within months I could play along with simple songs like 'Rocky Raccoon' and 'Cry Baby Cry'. The chords in these songs were relatively easy, in the sense that there were no barre chords, which I hadn't yet mastered due to the enormous strength you needed for them; especially taking into account that I was learning to play on my mother's Egmond guitar from the sixties, which over the course of time had gotten such a crooked neck that I could barely push a string onto the frets.

"I was totally blown away by the sheer versatility of the songs on The White Album, going from folk to almost heavy metal, to 1920s vaudeville, to straight rock 'n' roll. This album totally consumed all of my musical interest and energy for maybe a year or so.

"I had already been playing the piano for a couple of years, so some time went in to figuring out how to play songs like 'Martha My Dear' and 'Sexy Sadie'. They were rhythmically challenging enough to keep me busy, trying to get the vocal and piano parts exactly right.

"As my guitar playing, especially my finger-picking, got better, I managed to "master" songs like 'Dear Prudence', 'Happiness is a Warm Gun' and 'Mother Nature's Son'; but the real knockout for me was, of course, 'Blackbird'.

"From the moment I first heard it, I was mesmerized by the intricate weave of the singing melody, the bassline and the top line going in perfect counterpoint, and then this hypnotizing drone note that was constantly present underneath. As the whole album probably did on a broader level, this song, in particular, has defined my musicianship. I guess everyone has their song that determines, defines and colours their lives from the moment that

Right: In one of their last UK TV appearances, the Beatles performed 'Hey Jude' on David Frost's *Frost on Sunday* show in September 1968.

"It was the big tension album. For The White Album we were all in the middle of the psychedelic thing or just coming out of it. It was weird. Never before had we recorded with people visiting for hours on end and business meetings."

Paul McCartney (*Abbey Road*)

"After *Sgt. Pepper* the new album felt more like a band recording together."

"I remember having three studios operating at the same time: Paul was doing some overdubs in one, John was in another and I was recording some horns or something in a third."

George Harrison (*The Beatles Anthology*)

"I agree we should have put it out as two separate albums: the 'White' and the 'Whiter' album."

Ringo Starr (*The Beatles Anthology*)

Left: George Harrison (second right) stands with Ringo Starr and actress Jane Birkin at the Cannes Film Festival, where the film *Wonderwall* was premiered in May 1968.

Above: The original poster artwork for the film *Wonderwall*, directed by Joe Massot.

Overleaf: The Rolling Stones *Rock 'n' Roll Circus* starred (L–R) John Entwistle, Keith Moon. Pete Townshend, John Lennon, Yoko Ono, Keith Richards, Mick Jagger, Brian Jones, Bill Wyman, Eric Clapton and Marianne Faithfull.

What the Critics Said

"The Beatles are still a really vibrant and 'together' beat group, as well as being the best songwriters of their generation."

Ray Connolly, *Evening Standard*, November 1968

"Well, the new Beatles album's here with 30 catchy little numbers for you to whistle on your way to work, glide round the Mecca to, swoon in your bedsit, dance to at the hoe-down, play down on the farm, revive the jive, stomp to at your local rock palace or sing on the way to Grosvenor Square."

Barry Miles, *International Times*, November 1968

"One of the most significant landmarks in their recording career since 'Love Me Do' ... presenting the sheer good, bad and ugly of their work to late October 1968."

Alan Smith, *NME*, 1968

"The album illustrates that the four members can each have their own direction under the artistic umbrella of the Beatles, pulling in different directions but never catapulting into anarchy."

Alan Walsh, *Melody Maker*, 1968

NME readers' letters in 1968 included one from Peter Lawrence saying, **"The Beatles' new LP is the greatest thing to come out of a recording studio in recent years."** In *Melody Maker* at the same time, reader Munro Teale stated, **"Today I am selling my eight**

Beatles LPs. Gone are the smiling faces delivering good tunes with melodic backing. Now we have to listen to monotonous, gimmicky-ridden, sensational trash."

"The best thing in pop since *Sgt. Pepper* ... musically there is beauty, horror, surprise, chaos, order."

Derek Jewell, *The Sunday Times*, November 1968

"Whatever else it is or isn't, it is the best album they have ever made, and only the Beatles are capable of making a better one. In short, it is the new Beatles record and it fulfils all our expectations of it."

Jann Wenner, *Rolling Stone*, December 1968

Above: Apple Records star Mary Hopkin replaced the Beatles at Number One with 'Those Were the Days' in 1968.

Opposite: John Lennon and Yoko Ono arrive at The Old Vic theatre in London to see his play *In His Own Write*.

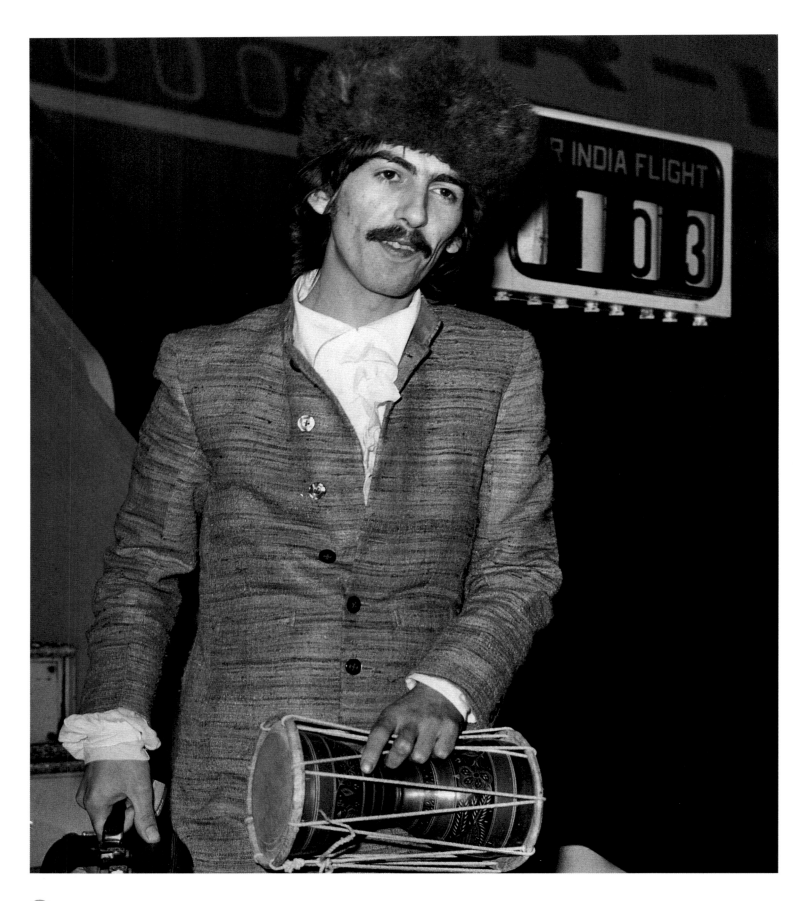

"There is almost no attempt in this new set to be anything but what the Beatles actually are: John, Paul, George and Ringo. Four different people, each with songs and styles and abilities."

Review, *Rolling Stone*, December 1968

"The Beatles' first album release on their new Apple label is without doubt their most ambitious and impressive to date. Of special interest is the packaging, which is a completely blank white cover."

Review, *Billboard* magazine, December 1968

Nik Cohn (*New York Times*, December 1968) described the songs as **"boring beyond belief"**, half of them **"profound mediocrities"**.

"Falling apart, [the Beatles] still made music that eclipsed most other groups."

Q magazine, 1986

"Amid band squabbling the Beatles produced *The Beatles*, an epic masterpiece that equals *Sgt Pepper*."

1001 Albums You Must Hear Before You Die

Above: (L–R) Ringo Starr, John Lennon, Paul McCartney and George Harrison hide among the flowers in the garden during a photo session at St Pancras Old Church.

Opposite: George Harrison returns to London after recording sessions in India in January 1968.

1969
Yellow Submarine

Yellow Submarine is listed as an official Beatles studio album although questions were raised at the time (and still are) as to whether it was a "proper" Beatles album. The debate centred around the fact that only six of the 13 tracks on the album actually featured the group and two of those had been issued some years earlier.

The film *Yellow Submarine* was a project Brian Epstein had agreed to when he negotiated the deal with United Artists that included the movies *A Hard Day's Night* and *Help!*. The Beatles were unenthusiastic about committing to, or appearing in, a third film and it fell to the American company King Features Syndicate to create the cartoon film.

King had signed a deal with Epstein to make and distribute in America a series of Beatles cartoon films featuring the band and their songs. Made by executive producer Al Brodax, the weekly half-hour films were aired in the USA by ABC TV from September 1965 until September 1969.

Brodax was then given the job of creating the Beatles' new cartoon feature film entitled *Yellow Submarine*, which featured the Beatles briefly and included four previously unreleased songs alongside the two earlier releases; and seven tracks composed and arranged by George Martin and performed by his orchestra.

Work on the title track began in May 1966 and finished on June 1, when sound effects – including a cash till, football rattles, chains, glasses and bells – were added. It was included on the album *Revolver* as Ringo Starr's vocal contribution and issued as the B-side of the Number One single 'Eleanor Rigby' in August 1966.

George Harrison's 'Only a Northern Song' was recorded in February and March 1967 as a possible track on *Sgt. Pepper* but was eventually discarded

Previous pages: A movie poster for *Yellow Submarine* (*Il Sottomarino Giallo*), Italy 1968.

Opposite: The premiere of *Yellow Submarine* at the London Pavilion, London, July 17, 1968.

Below: Paul and Linda McCartney pose with the police for photographers after their wedding in March 1969.

Yellow Submarine

Released January 17 1969 (Apple/Parlophone)

Yellow Submarine
Only a Northern Song
All Together Now
Hey Bulldog
It's All Too Much
All You Need Is Love
Pepperland
Sea of Time
Sea of Holes
Sea of Monsters
March of the Meanies
Pepperland Laid Waste
Yellow Submarine
 in Pepperland

Reached #3 in the UK, #1 in Canada and Norway, #4 in France, Germany and Australia, #5 in Norway and #2 in the USA.

and kept under wraps until the *Yellow Submarine* project came along.

'All Together Now' and 'It's All Too Much' were both recorded in May 1967 for the film soundtrack. 'All You Need Is Love', from the group's global satellite TV special, was recorded and broadcast in June 1967, when it was also released as a single.

The last song recorded for *Yellow Submarine* was 'Hey Bulldog', which John Lennon wrote and apparently declared, "It'll do for the film". It was completed in 10 hours on February 11, 1968 and fulfilled the Beatles' contribution to *Yellow Submarine*.

While he was still finishing work on The White Album in October 1968, George Martin spent two days at Abbey Road conducting his 41-piece orchestra. They re-recorded side two of the *Yellow Submarine* soundtrack, which Martin had taped the year before at Olympic Studios. At Abbey Road he shared the production with John Burgess and Ron Richards.

The album cover was designed by Czech-born graphic artist Heinz Edelmann and derived from images he had created in his role as the film's artistic director. The UK version of *Yellow Submarine* featured the words "Nothing is Real" under the title; and included a preview by *Observer* journalist Tony Palmer of The White Album, which was originally set for release soon afterwards.

In the end, the release of *Yellow Submarine* the album came six months after *Yellow Submarine* the film was premiered in London in July 1968. This was mainly because the Beatles wanted to focus attention on The White Album, which was issued in November 1968. The group also abandoned plans to release a five-track *Yellow Submarine* EP.

Yellow Submarine entered the UK chart in February and peaked at Number Three – the first "new" Beatles album not to reach Number One, although the group already held the top spot with The White Album.

Left: The four Beatles at TVC animation studios, participating in the *Mod Odyssey* documentary, November 6, 1967.

Tristan Fry

"I played on the *Yellow Submarine* album as part of the George Martin Orchestra, which was again a studio orchestra made up of session players. I remember doing that for two days in Studio 1 at Abbey Road; but again we didn't know what it was or who it was for.

"Ask anybody who did sessions back then and they will tell you the same, that they had no idea where what they were playing would end up. We could do four sessions a day in four different studios and not always know who they were for."

Ken Townsend

"I remember for [the track] 'Yellow Submarine' they wanted this particular sound and I put a small microphone with a plastic sleeve round it into a milk bottle full of water and they actually sang into a milk bottle to create the underwater sound effect.

"When we finished the track, Mal Evans [the Beatles' roadie] strapped this great big drum to his chest and everybody, including the Beatles, joined in a Hokey Cokey and went along the corridors into the canteen and back to the studio singing, 'We all live in a yellow submarine!' It was bit of end-session fun."

Tom Robinson

"'Yellow Submarine' is such an underwritten song – if it had been written with the same discipline as songs in the first few years, then it would have been a pub song forever.

"It's not a song – it's a band running out of ideas. I'm probably in a minority of one about this but I just think at the notepaper stage, when you're writing the lyrics down, that after writing down two verses and two choruses they got bored. It could have been a much better music hall, sing-around-the-piano-in-a-pub pop song."

Above: Ringo Starr and George Harrison with a Blue Meanie from *Yellow Submarine*, 1968.

Opposite: The happy couple – Paul and Linda McCartney after their London wedding.

- George Martin (*All You Need Is Ears*): "The film scraped the bottom of the Beatle music barrel as far as new material was concerned, the songs they produced being 'Only a Northern Song', 'All Together Now', 'Hey Bulldog' and 'It's All Too Much'."

- George Martin (*Daily Telegraph*, March 2016): "I think that one of the nice things about the *Yellow Submarine* movie is that it can be perennial. People enjoy watching from each generation. And it was like the Beatles themselves. You know the Beatles seem to find new audiences each time another generation comes along."

- Geoff Emerick (*Here, There and Everywhere*): "Both projects (*Magical Mystery Tour* and *Yellow Submarine*) were actually films and not albums. The main difference between the two was that the Beatles were completely uninterested in *Yellow Sub*, which was a feature-length cartoon that Brian Epstein had obligated them to do, apparently against their wishes. As a result it became a receptacle for any song of theirs that they deemed substandard, such as George Harrison's 'Only a Northern Song'."

- Tony Barrow (*John, Paul, George, Ringo & Me*): "In my opinion the most entertaining of the Beatles films – but not the most satisfactory from the musical point of view – was the one with which they were least involved, the innovative animation production *Yellow Submarine*. Initially unhappy about even lending their name to this film, the group's eventual half-hearted contribution consisted of providing some less-than-sensational songs and doing a brief 'epilogue' appearance at the end of the film."

What the Beatles Said

"It was the third movie that we owed United Artists. Brian [Epstein] had set it up and we had nothing to do with it. But I liked the movie: the artwork. They wanted another song so I knocked off 'Hey Bulldog'. It's a good-sounding record that means nothing."

John Lennon (*The Beatles Anthology*)

"Because they were going more in the *Pepper* direction, we said to use songs we'd already recorded like 'All You Need Is Love'."

Paul McCartney (*The Beatles Anthology*)

"There were albums which weren't any good as far as I was concerned, like *Yellow Submarine.*"

George Harrison (*Crawdaddy* magazine, 1977)

Opposite: Ringo Starr reflects on another photo session in front of the cameras.

Right: Paul and Linda McCartney cut a dash in a combination of stripes, tartan and polka dots.

What the Critics Said

"This is from the cartoon film and comprises two former Beatles singles hits – 'Yellow Submarine' and 'All You Need Is Love' – with four so-so songs written for the film and sung by the Beatles. The flip side has six compositions by George Martin, conducted by him for the film."

Allen Evans, *NME*, January 1969

(The *NME* gave the album a three-star rating and placed it second in their LP review section below Sergio Mendes' album *Fool on the Hill*, which was given four stars.)

"Beatle compositions and George Martin's film score from the cartoon. Great, but if you're short of readies better to get their new album."

Review, *Melody Maker*, January 1960

A review in *Record Mirror* said the release of *Yellow Submarine* would evoke **"the ecstasy of fans the world over"**. It added that the four new Beatles songs matched the quality of the two **"excellent"** hit singles, and Martin's side represented a **"tremendous achievement"**.

Beat Instrumental bemoaned the paucity of new material by the band, but added: **"Be not of bad cheer. The George Martin score to the film is really very nice, and two tracks by George Harrison redeem the first side. Both [songs] are superb pieces, considerably more enthralling than the most draggy, 'All Together Now', a rather wet track."**

"Featuring songs from their highly successful cartoon feature, this LP boasts four new Beatles songs (plus 'Yellow Submarine' and 'All You Need Is Love'), along with an intoxicating score by George Martin on side two."

Billboard magazine, January 1969

Opposite: Feet first from John Lennon during his 'bed-in for peace' in the Queen Elizabeth Hotel in Montreal in May 1969.

Below: Allen Klein took control of the Beatles' business empire in 1969.

1969
Abbey Road

Was *Abbey Road* the penultimate album produced by the Beatles or was it their final offering? The debate rages on. It was certainly the last album the group ever recorded together; but it was released as their 11th UK studio collection and another title, recorded earlier but delayed, would follow.

In fact when the Beatles returned to Abbey Road in January 1969, following the release of The White Album and *Yellow Submarine*, they worked concurrently on songs that would appear on their two final albums. That process would continue until July when they focused all their attention on *Abbey Road*.

At one point during this period George Harrison briefly quit the group, apparently disenchanted with talk of TV shows and live concerts. But he returned 12 days later and work resumed, starting with 'She Came In Through the Bathroom Window'. By mid-April the band had begun work on four more tracks and during this time George Martin handed over the producer's chair to both Glyn Johns and Chris Thomas. Recording took place at Trident Studios and Olympic Studios in addition to Abbey Road.

The Beatles also took time out on January 30 to give their final, unforgettable live performance, which they chose to play on the roof of their Apple offices and studio in London's Savile Row. They needed live performances of songs for their planned *Get Back* project and, as they were never going to tour again, a private/public show high above the streets of Mayfair was their compromise.

This was the period when the Beatles struggled to get control and ownership of Northern Songs Ltd, the music publishing company they had allowed to go public in February 1965 to alleviate their tax burden. Fellow founding directors Dick James and Charles Silver were intent on selling their 32 per cent share to ATV (Associated Television Corporation) while Lennon and McCartney tried to prevent it by outbidding the corporation. They failed. In December 1969 Northern Songs fell into the hands of ATV.

Abbey Road

Released September 26, 1969 (Apple/Parlophone)

Come Together

Something

Maxwell's Silver Hammer

Oh! Darling

Octopus's Garden

I Want You (She's So Heavy)

Here Comes the Sun

Because

You Never Give Me Your Money

Sun King

Mean Mr Mustard

Polythene Pam

She Came In Through the Bathroom Window

Golden Slumbers

Carry That Weight

The End

Her Majesty

Reached #1 in the UK, Australia, Canada, France, Germany, Norway, thr USA, Holland and Sweden and peaked at #3 in Japan. Apart from the retrospective compilation album, *1*, it is the bestselling Beatles album of all time with 14.4 million sales; and it is #14 on *Rolling Stone's* 500 Greatest Albums of All Time.

Previous pages: The Beatles pictured crossing Abbey Road on a giant advertising billboard on Los Angeles' Sunset Strip.

Left: The McCartney family – (L–R) Linda, Heather and Paul – arrive in New York after their London wedding.

Opposite: John Lennon and Yoko Ono took their campaign for World Peace to Montreal in May 1969.

After taking the whole of June off, the Beatles stepped back into the studio in July 1969 and stayed there until 'I Want You (She's So Heavy)' brought the recording of *Abbey Road* to an end on August 20, 1969. That date has gone down in history as the last time all four Beatles were together in the studio that had played such a huge part in their success.

As *Abbey Road* neared completion, the minor detail of a title and sleeve design for the new release arose. So on August 8 the band took time out for a photo shoot on the pedestrian crossing in front of the studios in Abbey Road, London NW8. The photographer was Iain Macmillan, who had worked with Yoko Ono. She subsequently introduced him to John Lennon, who in turn invited him to photograph the group's new album cover.

The fact that McCartney wore no shoes for some of the shots of him on the crossing, coupled with a random Volkswagen Beetle being parked in the background with a number plate ending 281F, led some fans and conspiracy theorists to speculate that the Beatles bass player was dead. They calculated that he would have been "28 IF he was alive" – and that he had been replaced by a McCartney lookalike.

In fact the car belonged to a local resident who always parked his car on the street in front of the studio – in the days before yellow lines, parking meters and wardens. McCartney was actually 27 when the album cover photo session took place.

Abbey Road went straight to Number One in the UK in October, replacing Blind Faith's titular album, and stayed there for 11 weeks: exactly the same length of time it held the top spot in America. The Rolling Stones had a week in the top spot with *Let It Bleed*, but then it was the Beatles' turn again for another six of the album's 81-week stint on the UK chart. It was the second-longest run of any of the Beatles' original studio albums.

Opposite: John Lennon and the Plastic Ono Band on stage at London's Lyceum Ballroom.

Below: George Harrison on tour with Delaney & Bonnie & Friends in December 1969.

stuck out for me was the production: it was just absolutely fantastic. Some of the earlier albums had sort of been thrown together but were still brilliant, but *Abbey Road* was just like a polished gem. It was fabulous.

"That was the key thing that stood out for me. The brilliance and cleverness of just piecing bits and bobs of songs together. The way they meld them all together is just amazing – you're talking different keys and tempos and feels and everything but they glue it all together with Beatles magic.

"That was when George Harrison really came to the forefront. Without his contributions there isn't really a great deal by way of singles or actual complete songs you can choose from. They are the stand-out tracks on the album as records that work from start to finish.

"It is a fitting finale to their time together and the fact that it ends on 'The End' is quite poignant. They must have known it was the end, even if nobody actually admitted it. The whole thing, with the cover, is just fantastic.

Ken Townsend

"*Abbey Road* is an album I like – it's one of their best albums and some of the songs are wonderful. I was there for some of those sessions as I was in charge of the technical department.

"In actual fact *Abbey Road* has got to be my favourite Beatles album because I renamed EMI Recording Studios Abbey Road as a result of that album. I did that in 1976. We were known as Abbey Road but were not officially registered as that. EMI insisted that the EMI logo and name was still on the door but [said] we could use the name Abbey Road as well. We took it as a great compliment that the Beatles should choose to name what turned out to be their last album after our studio."

Glen Matlock

"There's a few rockers on it I like but [Side Two's] a bit weird with that medley thing – 'What's all that about?' went through my mind when I first heard it."

Opposite: Peter Sellers and Ringo Starr enjoy the celebrations at the end of the filming party for *The Magic Christian*.

Right, above: George Harrison produced the Radha Krishna Temple's top 20 hit single in 1969.

Right: Paul and Linda McCartney go past the dustbins and in through a side door for their wedding at Marylebone Register Office.

- Iain Macmillan (interviewed by the author 1981): "I got the job through John but it was Paul's idea and I was given 10 minutes to do it. It was a nerve-racking experience. I had never met all four Beatles together before that day. I had to climb up a stepladder in the middle of the road to take the shot and a friendly policeman held up the traffic for me.

  "Paul turned up in his Oxfam suit and sandals and because it was a hot day he decided to do some shots with sandals on and some with sandals off. Paul checked all the pictures with a magnifying glass – I don't think the other three were particularly bothered. He chose the neatest shot with the legs stretched in almost uniform style and it was pure coincidence that it happened to be with his sandals off."

- George Martin (interviewed by the author, 1981): "I didn't think we'd work again after *Let It Be* and I didn't really want to; and when Paul rang me up and they wanted me to come in and produce another record, I said 'I've been there Paul and I don't like it, I don't think I want to do this.' But we all got back into the studio again and John was honey pie. I knew it was the end and they knew it was the end but they were coming back for one final stab at doing something really worthwhile together before they went off into the sunset and their own particular ways."

- George Martin (*Daily Telegraph*, March 2016): "I've got quite a few favourite Beatles albums. I like *Revolver* very much and I like *Rubber Soul* very much, but I'm very fond of *Abbey Road*. Probably because it's the last album we made and we kind of knew that.

  "There was an inexplicable presence when all four were together in a room. Their music was bigger than they were."

- Alan Parsons (interviewed by the author): "My title was assistant engineer and one of the things I was told to do after the *Let It Be* sessions was the *Abbey Road* sessions. The idea was that it was the return to the studio to make another exciting studio album as least as good as *Sgt. Pepper*. But one thing they didn't want to do was spend the same amount of time and *Abbey Road* was recorded in a total of eight weeks – considerably less time than *Sgt. Pepper*.

  "I think there was a general atmosphere of finality – the ladies (Yoko and Linda) were on the scene – and you could sense the tension between John and Paul. And the tension was obviously demonstrated by the fact that they would very rarely appear together on the same day.

  "It was a fairly solitary experience – a bit like doing a solo Beatles album that turned into a compilation at the end."

- Alicia Keys (*Complex.com*): "[The Beatles] have this way of creating something simple and deep at the same time. Something easy and complex simultaneously is actually mind-blowing – how good they are! This album is surely one of my faves."

- Ian Prowse (*Liverpool Echo*, September 2009): "Then at the very end of an unimaginably creative eight-year period with a band torn apart by diverging interests and the ever-painful stress of actually growing up, they only went and made their best album, *Abbey Road*. And don't get me started on how good the cover is."

- Geoff Emerick (*Here, There and Everywhere*): "In contrast to the mayhem that was The White Album, the atmosphere during the making of the *Abbey Road* album was quite muted. Everyone seemed to be walking on eggshells, trying not to offend. Looking back it seems to me that the Beatles were all on their best behaviour because they were determined to turn in a good album after the disaster that was *Let It Be*.

  "During the *Abbey Road* sessions, it never occurred to me that we were working on the last Beatles album. Of course I realized that they were growing apart and arguing a lot but they were also still making great music together ... and they were still clearly a going commercial success."

- Pete Brown (*The Love You Make*): "This album turned out to be the last of the Beatles' masterpieces, with most of the 17 cuts a group effort, truly a minor miracle."

- Mickie Most (*Abbey Road*): "*Abbey Road* has remained part of the tradition of the record business and one of the best albums ever made was called *Abbey Road* and you can't get a better advert than that."

- Cliff Richard (*Abbey Road*): "The rock 'n' roll scene put Abbey Road on the map and the Beatles album, of course, clinched it."

- Tony Barrow (*John, Paul, George, Ringo & Me*): "George Martin's assessment of *Abbey Road* was that 'one side was very much what John wanted and the second side was what Paul and I wanted'."

Previous pages: George Harrison backs up Eric Clapton during the Delaney & Bonnie & Friends European tour in 1969.

Opposite: George Harrison enjoying life on the road without the Beatles in 1969.

What the Beatles Said

"After the *Let It Be* nightmare, *Abbey Road* turned out fine. The second side is brilliant. Out of the ashes of all the madness, that last section for me is one of the finest pieces of music we put together."

Ringo Starr (*The Beatles Anthology*)

"There were one or two tense moments but I was getting into a lot of musical ideas; the medley on the second side – I was really up on that.

    "As I remember it we were in Studio three and kinda said 'Why don't we call it *Abbey Road* and why don't we have a picture of us on the crossing outside?'. It was the simplest thing to do. It is *Abbey Road* and for everyone who didn't know the name of the studio, that would imply something kinda mystical."

Paul McCartney (*Abbey Road*)

"But that was *Abbey Road*. We had the cover, we had the title, we had all the music and it came out before *Let It Be*. I think it worked out OK as an album. I think John thought in the end it was a bit slick – but I don't think it was bad for that. That's just structure. I don't think it really looks slick now."

Paul McCartney (*The Beatles Anthology*)

Previous pages: John Lennon and Yoko Ono after returning his MBE to Buckingham Palace in November 1969.

Right: Just five days after their wedding John Lennon and Yoko Ono began their 'bed-in' at the Amsterdam Hilton Hotel in March 1969.

"I like some of the tracks and I don't like other tracks. *Abbey Road* was a competent album. I don't think it was anything more than that or anything else."

John Lennon (*The Beatles Anthology*)

"I liked the A-side but I never liked the sort of pop opera in the other side. I think it's junk because it's just bits of songs thrown together. It was a competent album like *Rubber Soul*. It was together in that way but *Abbey Road* had no life in it."

John Lennon (*Rolling Stone*, 1970)

"I didn't know at the time that it was the last Beatle record that we would make, but it felt as if we were reaching the end of the line. There were plenty of other activities to fill the gaps. I was certainly not missing being in the band."

George Harrison (*The Beatles Anthology*)

Above: Yoko Ono and John Lennon enjoy a working lunch at the Beatles' Apple offices.

Opposite: Paul and Linda McCartney dressed up for the opening of the film *Isadora* starring Vanessa Redgrave.

What the Critics Said

Richard Williams (*Melody Maker*, September 1969, on An Evening With John and Yoko at the New Cinema Club at London's ICA): **"The star of the evening was undoubtedly the Beatles' new album *Abbey Road* which was played during the intermission. The music it contains is not self-consciously a regression – as was the case with *Get Back* and much of the double [*White*] album – but rather, it related to the pre-*Sgt. Pepper* days of *Rubber Soul*. If you still dig *Rubber Soul* and *Revolver* you'll dote on *Abbey Road*."**

"A vast improvement on their last album, being far more concise and positive. Undoubtedly the least pretentious set from them in a long while, even to the cover, which is refreshingly 'straight'.

Review, *Melody Maker*, September 1969

"Material, all new, is potent and commercial with the spotlight on the single 'Something'. Clever, typical Beatles material."

Review, *Billboard* magazine, October 1969

"Side two does more for me than the whole of *Sgt. Pepper*, and I'll trade you *The Beatles* and *Magical Mystery Tour* and a Keith Moon drumstick for Side one."

John Mendelsohn (*Rolling Stone*, November 1969)

Opposite: Jonh Lennon and Yoko Ono launch the worldwide posters for their War Is Over campaign in December 1969.

Below: Newly-weds Linda and Paul McCartney arrive home after their London wedding.

Overleaf: John Lennon and Yoko Ono face the media with Allen Klein (left) at the offices of Apple.

JOHN AND
YOKO'S
T.V. FILM
BRILLIANT

EVENING
STANDARD

"Often neglected in Beatles' all-time best album polls in favour of more technicolor *Sgt. Pepper* ... and the darker, less orthodox *Revolver*, the Beatles' last recorded album is a shimmering, never predictable array of songs and song fragments. It is as progressive as anything the quartet ever recorded."

1001 Albums You Must Hear Before You Die

"It's beautiful, blistering music ... it's something of *Revolver* ... it's something all its own ... it exceeds the double [White] album and parts of it touch the heights of *Sgt. Pepper*. [The] album is always brilliant and only occasionally fair."

Allan Smith, *NME*, September 1969

"The disc proves lucky indeed – for listeners who like being disarmed by the world's four most fortunate and famous music makers. Melodic, inventive, crammed with musical delights, *Abbey Road* is the best thing the Beatles have done since *Sgt. Pepper*. Whereas that historic record stretched the ear and challenged the mind and imagination, *Abbey Road* is a return to the modest, pre-*Pepper* style of *Rubber Soul* and *Revolver*. It has a cheerful coherence – each song's mood fits comfortably with every other – and a sense of wholeness clearly contrived as a revel in musical pleasure."

Time magazine, October 1969

Left: John Lennon's final British concert appearance was at the Lyceum Ballroom in London on December 15, 1969.

1970
Let It Be

Let It Be

Released May 8, 1970
(Apple/Parlophone)

Two of Us

Dig a Pony

Across the Universe

I Me Mine

Dig It

Let It Be

Maggie Mae

I've Got A Feeling

One After 909

The Long and Winding
Road

For You Blue

Get Back

Reached # 1 in the
UK, Australia, Canada,
Netherlands, Norway
and the USA, peaked
at #2 in Japan and
Sweden, #3 in Germany
and #5 in France. 'Let
It Be' was awarded the
1971 Academy Award
for Best Original Song
Score.

What started out as an idea for a worldwide television special under the banner *Get Back*, featuring the Beatles performing live, eventually became the group's final album and a feature film, both entitled *Let It Be*.

The idea for a concert and TV special came from McCartney but the rest of the group were unenthusiastic, so much so that Harrison briefly left the group in protest. Despite this setback the sessions for the album began in January 1969, alongside sessions for *Abbey Road*, in their own Apple Studio in Savile Row, where they worked on 'All I Want Is You' (the working title for 'Dig a Pony') and 'I've Got a Feeling'.

The band recorded classic rock 'n' roll tracks alongside original songs by Lennon, McCartney and Harrison with American keyboard player Billy Preston joining them in the studio. When they finished in the Apple Studio in early February 1969, the Beatles moved on to Trident, Olympic and Abbey Road Studios before breaking off to focus on tracks for the *Abbey Road* album.

On Saturday January 3, 1970 the Beatles made their last ever recording in Abbey Road, although as John Lennon was holidaying in Denmark only three of the group were there. It was left to McCartney, Harrison and Starr to finish off the *Get Back* album and record 'I Me Mine', which brought to an end the band's long association with the studio they first visited in June 1962.

While George Martin had featured as producer on all the *Get Back* sessions, the final tapes were given to Glyn Johns, who had acted as engineer on the recordings, to compile into a last album. Johns, who had worked with the Rolling Stones, Georgie Fame, the Who, Traffic and the Kinks, came up with a 16-track master tape – including 'Save the Last

Previous pages: The film *Let It Be* opened at the London Pavilion cinema on May 20, 1970 – and no Beatles attended.

Above: Police join forces to control Beatles fans at the premiere of the film *Let It Be*.

Opposite: George Harrison learnt how to master the sitar from the Indian musician Ravi Shankar.

Dance for Me', 'Rocker' and 'Don't Let Me Down' – which remains unreleased.

Despite the release of the single 'Let It Be' on March 6, the Beatles were on the brink of splitting up and planning their various solo debuts while their final recordings remained under wraps. At the same time, American manager and music publisher Allen Klein took over as the band's business manager and, in order to finish what they had started, he suggested hiring legendary record producer Phil Spector.

Famous for his 'Wall of Sound' recordings with Ike and Tina Turner, the Ronettes and the Righteous Brothers, Spector replaced Martin and Johns. Between March 23 and April 2, he took the *Get Back* tapes and turned them into *Let It Be* at Abbey Road Studio. His work on McCartney's songs 'Let It Be' and 'The Long and Winding Road' in particular, when he added a choir, strings and brass, caused the biggest stir with the Beatles bass player, who complained that he had not been consulted or given any opportunity to hear Spector's treatment of his songs before they were released.

Let It Be, with Spector credited as 'reproducer', was issued on May 8, 1970. Its cover featured four individual portraits of the Beatles, taken by Ethan Russell, surrounded by a black border (the same design was used for 'Let It Be' the single). The album was initially packaged in a box together with a 160-page booklet of pictures and text; but in November that year a version without the box and booklet was released.

Two weeks after the release of the album, the film *Let It Be*, directed by Michael Lindsay-Hogg, was released in cinemas around the world. It documented the Beatles rehearsing in Twickenham Studios in early 1969, recording at their basement studio at the Apple headquarters in Savile Row and performing their final, unannounced concert on the roof. It won the group the Best Original Song Score Oscar in 1971.

Let It Be entered the UK album chart at Number One in May and held on to the top spot for three weeks, the shortest run for any Beatles album, before being replaced by Simon & Garfunkel's *Bridge Over Troubled Water*. In America *Let It Be* knocked *McCartney*, the debut solo offering from Paul McCartney, off the top spot and stayed there for four weeks before being replaced by the *Woodstock* soundtrack album.

Opposite: Ringo Starr and Raquel Welch share a scene in the film *The Magic Christian*.

Below: Fans gather outside the Beatles' Apple offices in Savile Row, London.

Graham Gouldman

"*Let It Be* is no slouch as an album even though it was an unhappy album – it did have 'The Long and Winding Road' and 'Across the Universe' – but I do have a problem about even criticising the Beatles, it's a kind of unconditional love."

Barbara Dickson

"'Across the Universe' is one of the best songs I have ever heard – it is the most wonderful song. I love the words – it's so abstract, so beautiful, so transcendental, it relaxes everybody who either plays it or listens to it. The public don't really like 'Across the Universe' at all – they are not remotely interested in it but I don't care about that – it's what I like that I sing and play and it works for me."

Glen Matlock

"Not their best album."

Above: John Lennon's collection of lithographs were removed by the police in 1970 under the Obscene Publications Act.

Left: Phil Spector, who was hired to 're-produce' the album *Let It Be*.

Opposite: George Harrison has come a long way from the days of the 'mop-top' Beatles.

Overleaf: Maureen and Ringo Starr, who wears a well-placed plug for his latest film.

- Alan Parsons (interviewed by the author): "The *Let It Be* sessions were the first time I encountered all four Beatles and George Martin; and it was not at Abbey Road but at the Beatles' own Savile Row studio. I was sent down to help salvage their studio and it was a brilliant bonus to be one of the last people to see them playing together as a band live for the very last time."

- George Martin (interviewed by the author): "And *Let It Be* became torture because John's premise was to take a song, rehearse it, get it right and record it – but they never got it right. And when I heard that John and George had taken the tapes out of Abbey Road and given them to Phil Spector to make them work, I felt a betrayal, really.

  "And when the record came to be issued, EMI rang up and said they didn't want my name on the record, it would be produced by Phil Spector. I said, 'But I produced all the original stuff that they worked on.' I told them I was not having that and suggested, 'Why don't you put on it, "produced by George Martin, overproduced by Phil Spector?"' But they didn't seem to go for that."

- George Martin (*The Beatles Anthology*): "*Let It Be* was such an unhappy record (even though there are some great songs on it) that I really believed that was the end of the Beatles and I assumed I would never work with them again."

- Engineer Glyn Johns (interviewed by the BBC, 1981): "I cannot bring myself to listen to the Phil Spector version of the album. I heard a few bars of it once and was totally disgusted and I think it's an absolute load of garbage."

- Elvis Costello (*Rolling Stone*): "Their breakup album, *Let It Be*, contains songs both gorgeous and jagged. I remember going to Leicester Square and seeing the film of *Let It Be* in 1970. I left with a melancholy feeling."

- Pete Brown (*The Love You Make*): "Spector had completely bastardized the Beatles sound. Although it had certain merits, *Let It Be* was purely a Phil Spector Wall of Sound production, with his inimitable backdrop of vast choruses and lavish orchestrations."

- Tony Bramwell (*Magical Mystery Tour*): "John and George were keen on Phil Spector and when Allen Klein, who was busy trying to please them, asked them who could rescue these tapes, they suggested Phil. In the spring of 1970 Phil smothered the lot with strings, horns and female choruses and it was released as *Let It Be*.

  "When Phil (Spector) came over to rescue the *Let It Be* recordings, which had gone horribly wrong and which the Beatles had lost all interest in, we had to sort through hundreds of tapes stacked up all over the place, offcuts of music and hours of conversation from shooting the film. Phil carted them all off to Abbey Road and holed up for months while he worked."

What the Critics Said

"If the Beatles soundtrack album *Let It Be* is to be their last then it will stand as a cheapskate epitaph, a cardboard tombstone, a sad and tatty end to a musical fusion which wiped clean and drew again the face of pop music.

"At £3.00 – bar a penny – can this mini-collection of new tracks, narcissistic pin-ups and chocolate-box dressing really be the last will and testament of the once respected and most famous group in the world?

"I have followed, vaunted and glowed with Mersey pride at the achievements of the Beatles since the pre-'Love Me Do' days of the Blue Angel and New Brighton Tower. But in its overwrapped state, this glorified EP is a bad and sad mistake."

Alan Smith, *NME*, May 1970

"The short note on the sleeve of *Let It Be* claims that this is a 'new phase Beatles album'. Looking at it, as we must, from the perspective of more than a year after it was recorded, nothing could be further from the truth.

"It has the feel of early Beatles, of the era before *Rubber Soul* almost, when the complexities were still natural and the possibilities of the recording studio comparatively unexplored. It also has the appearance of an epitaph …

"A beautiful thing to own, then, but it already has the feeling of finality about it, as if you are holding the

Above: Concerned fans read all about the Beatles' split outside the Apple offices in London's Savile Row.

Opposite above: Phil Spector with George Harrison during the *Let It Be* sessions.

Opposite below: Ringo Starr and Maureen Starr on the set of NBC's TV show *Laugh-In,* with (L–R) Miss Vicki, her husband Tiny Tim and actress Carol Channing.

last document from the collective personality known as the Beatles."

Richard Williams, *Melody Maker*, May 1970

"Somebody apparently just couldn't *Let It Be*, with the result that they put the load on their new friend P Spector, who in turn whipped out his orchestra and choir and proceeded to turn several of the rough gems on the best Beatles album in years into costume jewellery. To Phil Spector, stinging slaps on both wrists."

Ed Ward, *Rolling Stone*, June 1970

"The Beatles' latest LP serves as the soundtrack of the forthcoming film *Let It Be* and, as produced by Phil Spector, gives the impression of a 'live' performance."

Review, *Billboard* magazine, May 1970

"A last will and testament, from the blackly funereal packaging to the music itself, which sums up so much of what the Beatles as artists have been – unmatchably brilliant at their best, careless and self-indulgent at their least."

Derek Jewell, *The Sunday Times*, May 1970

"Oops. The Beatles had quietly broken up before their final album was released, the soundtrack to a rather disheartening documentary in which discomfort between the principle players is all too apparent.

"A slight, sad postscript, there are still monster tunes here by anyone else's standards but it lacks some clarity and is peppered with underdeveloped, substandard titles."

Neil McCormick, *Daily Telegraph*, September 2009

Above: Maureen and Ringo Starr join forces for yet another press interview.

Opposite: George Harrison's music for the film *Wonderwall* was the first album to be released on the Beatles own Apple label.

Back in the USA

The Beatles' American LP Releases

by Kenneth Womack

During the Beatles' heyday – as the group released one classic album after another to the waiting world – stateside listeners experienced Beatlemania in a decidedly different fashion than their British counterparts.

From the release of *Meet the Beatles!* in January 1964 through the *Hey Jude* compilation in February 1970 and beyond, the band's US records were markedly dissimilar from their official UK catalogue, which had been released on EMI's Parlophone label since October 1962. There were clearly economic factors in play: as EMI's American subsidiary, Capitol Records worked with an understandable zeal to drive as much product as possible into the hands of consumers during the heady days after the group's triumphant appearance on *The Ed Sullivan Show* in February 1964.

By carving up the Beatles' UK releases into a series of repackaged LPs, Capitol honed a strategy that allowed the record company to release new Beatles product into the US marketplace at a rate of every two to five months, a clip that far outpaced the group's British output during the same period. In so doing, they created dozens of unique entries in the Beatles' discography – many of which have since been deleted – that lingered until 1987, when EMI consolidated the band's official catalogue around the original UK releases.

The anomalous nature of the Beatles' American releases originated from longstanding bureaucratic issues at Capitol Records that led to a significant delay in the onset of Beatlemania in the USA, as well as in terms of the manner in which American fans originally experienced the albums. Originally founded in 1942 by Johnny Mercer, Buddy DeSylva, and Glenn Wallichs, Capitol had emerged as North America's premier West Coast label by the early 1950s.

During that same period, Sir Joseph Lockwood had been appointed as Chairman of the EMI Group with a clear mandate to stave off bankruptcy and turn the struggling record conglomerate's fortunes around. In one of his earliest moves, Lockwood spearheaded EMI's $8.5-million buyout

in January 1955 of Capitol Records, the American juggernaut. The British music press saw the move as a harbinger for EMI's British recordings to enjoy a more expansive American marketplace. As the *Melody Maker* reported, "A new field is open for a greater distribution than ever before of EMI 'popular' records in America."

Yet as part of the deal with EMI, Capitol ensured that the Hollywood-based label preserved its standing right to refuse to release UK acts unless Capitol execs felt that they could succeed stateside. The clause, already infamous among EMI's A&R men, was known as the "first turn-down option." And, more often than not, the folks back in Hollywood did just that, having dismissed the vast majority of British records as being altogether incongruous with what they perceived to be a distinctly American sound.

As it happened, the latter issue was the least of Sir Joseph's concerns. At the time, his primary motive was to increase EMI's profit margin, of course. But he was also keenly interested in acquiring Capitol as a means for ensuring that EMI controlled the American company's means of production – its massive manufacturing centres in Scranton, Pennsylvania, and Hollywood, California.

Shortly after concluding the Capitol buyout, Sir Joseph commissioned a new building to serve as the subsidiary's headquarters. Completed in April 1956, the Capitol Records building quickly emerged as one of Hollywood's most distinctive landmarks, given the 13-storey tower's iconic circular design. The building also featured a state-of-the-art recording studio that rivalled – if not exceeded at the time – the technological capabilities of EMI [later Abbey Road] Studios in London's St John's Wood.

Previous pages: All four Beatles enjoy the sights in America's capital city Washington DC, in February 1964.

Opposite: Ringo, Paul and John with a horse and carriage in New York's Central Park, February 10, 1964. George was back at the Plaza Hotel with a sore throat.

Below: A ticket for the opening show of the Beatles' 1965 tour at New York's Shea Stadium.

SID BERNSTEIN, Presents

RAIN CHECK — SEE REVERSE SIDE

SHEA STADIUM
ENTER GATE A
UPPER BOX $5.65
32 814A 6
SEC. BOX SEAT
SUN. AUG. 15, 1965-8 P.M.

All in all, Sir Joseph's acquisition proved to be a bold move, with Capitol increasing its dominion in the American record industry in short order. By the early 1960s, the EMI Group had secured its place as an international juggernaut, even going so far as to challenge Decca to become the UK's largest record company.

When it came to the Beatles, Decca registered an early black mark in the band's history when the company famously dropkicked an opportunity to sign the Fab Four. Decca was not alone, of course. The Beatles' circuitous pathway to success had claimed a number of victims. In 1975, the group's first manager Allan Williams entitled his autobiography *The Man Who Gave the Beatles Away*. In so doing, he recognized his own complicity in failing to capitalize on the band's budding musical genius – a role that fell in November 1961 to Brian Epstein, the eventual architect of Beatlemania.

But Williams was only the first in a long line of gatekeepers who failed to recognize the Beatles' greatness. Up next was Dick Rowe, the head A&R man for Decca Records. Rowe notoriously passed on signing the Beatles after their January 1962 audition, infamously saying, "groups with guitars are on the way out". As time has so brutally demonstrated, Rowe's powers of prognostication were grossly mistaken.

However, when it comes to neglecting to appreciate the group's early potential, Rowe is rivalled only by Dave E. Dexter Jr., the longtime Capitol Records employee who steadfastly refused to release the Beatles' runaway British hits stateside. In later years, when American Beatlemania reached its apex, Dexter was instrumental in repackaging the Beatles for the American marketplace, cannibalizing their original UK releases and adding large doses of reverb to alter their sound.

Opposite: (L–R) John Lennon, Paul McCartney and Ringo Starr – George Harrison was sick – take in the sites in New York's Central Park in February 1964.

Below: The Beatles onstage in America in 1964 when they played 30 concerts in 25 cities in one month.

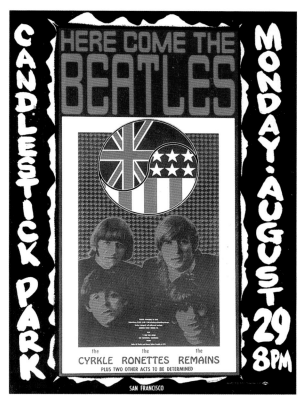

Born in Kansas City in 1915, Dexter began his career as a music journalist in the 1930s and 1940s with the *Kansas City Journal Post* and later with *Down Beat* magazine. A jazz aficionado with a well-honed ear, Dexter produced an album entitled *Kansas City Jazz* that traced the history of the local jazz scene through the work of such artists as Count Basie and Big Joe Turner. In 1943, Dexter joined fledgling Capitol Records as a publicity officer, eventually becoming the company's influential international A&R representative. During this period he attracted a number of celebrated artists to Capitol including Frank Sinatra, Peggy Lee, Stan Kenton, Nat King Cole, Duke Ellington and Woody Herman.

In terms of his production work, Dexter achieved considerable renown for his efforts behind the creation of Duke Ellington jazz standard *Satin Doll*. In 1946, he flexed his journalistic muscles and became a fully fledged author, publishing *Jazz Cavalcade: The Inside Story*

Left: Thank you and goodbye – The Beatles leave Candlestick Park in San Francisco after their last ever concert in August 1966.

Above: A poster advertising what was to be the Beatles' final concert.

of Jazz. He later authored *The Jazz Story from the '90s to the '60s* (1964), which jazz historian Floyd Levin described as "one of the most valuable jazz reference works available".

In Levin's estimation, Dexter made his mark as one of the industry's greatest jazz record producers: "Dave Dexter's crowning achievement was *The History of Jazz*, a series of four 78 RPM albums he produced for Capitol Records in 1944. He conceived the idea, assembled the impressive array of musicians, and personally supervised the entire project. To this day, those great recordings remain among the most ambitious anthologies of jazz history."

In addition to his pioneering work in cultivating the label's jazz interests, Dexter established a world music series entitled *Capitol of the World*, while editing the company's in-house publication *Capitol News*. Yet by the 1950s, Dexter began to deride the shifting demographics in popular music, particularly with the rise of rock 'n' roll artists such as Elvis Presley, whom he described as "juvenile and maddeningly repetitive".

By the early 1960s, Dexter's influence at Capitol Records had become so significant that company president Alan W. Livingston authored a June 1962 memo in which he instructed his colleagues to submit all import albums for Dexter's express consideration and approval. It was under these auspices that he passed on a series of options to release import records by Capitol's parent company, the EMI Group.

In October 1962, Dexter opted not to release the Beatles' 'Love Me Do' single, following suit in early 1963 with 'Please Please Me' and 'From Me to You', which were subsequently released by Vee-Jay Records. Soon after that, Dexter passed on the option to release 'She Loves You', which had emerged as the UK's bestselling single of all time at that juncture. 'She Loves You' was subsequently optioned by Philadelphia's Swan Records.

During this period, Epstein and George Martin engaged in a concerted letter-writing campaign in which they beseeched Capitol to take note of the Beatles' unparalleled UK success. But their pleas came to no avail, falling time after time on the ears

Above: In July 1976 John Lennon won his court case to stay in America when he was granted a "green card" visa.

Opposite: (L–R) John Lennon, Paul McCartney, George Harrison and Ringo Starr take a yacht out for a trip around Miami in February 1964.

of Dexter, who refused to budge from his initial reaction to the group's sound.

In a 1988 interview, Dexter recalled the first time that he heard the Beatles' 'Please Please Me.' "The British companies – they wanted us to issue as many of their records over here as possible because [the United States] was the biggest record market in the world. And I can only remember when I heard Lennon playing the harmonica on this record I thought it was the worst thing I'd ever heard."

The landscape changed in a hurry, though, after EMI racked up nearly 300,000 advance orders for *With The Beatles* in the autumn of 1963. EMI could simply no longer wait for its American subsidiary to come around. Livingston and Capitol Records were subsequently ordered by EMI's managing director LG Wood to release the Beatles' next single without delay. With the band slated to perform on *The*

Ed Sullivan Show on February 9, 1964, American promoter Sid Bernstein signed them for a pair of shows at Carnegie Hall that same week.

Having originally planned to press a mere 5,000 copies of 'I Want to Hold Your Hand', Capitol earmarked the impressive sum of $40,000 to promote the single in the United States, and American Beatlemania was born.

In later years, Dexter begrudgingly acknowledged the commercial quality of 'I Want to Hold Your Hand' saying, "I heard about four bars of that and I grabbed it. I knew it was the Beatles; [and] Capitol recovered the mighty Beatles quartet." Dexter was shocked by the single's roaring success. Indeed, Capitol Records was so overrun by the record-buying public's massive appetite for the Beatles that "by New Year, we had to have RCA press Capitol records. It was that big."

As evidenced by internal Capitol Records memos collected in Dexter's archive at the University of Missouri-Kansas City, the fallout from Dexter's tardiness in making the Beatles a priority for Capitol Records was rather swift. On February 7, 1964, Lloyd Dunn, Vice President of Merchandising and Sales for Capitol, instructed Dexter to send him any records that the A&R representative had decided to reject under the guise, in Dunn's words, of needing "to better familiarize myself with foreign product".

In February, Dexter defended himself in a memo to Livingston, writing: "Alan, I make errors in judgment as does everyone else, but when you consider the enormous amount of singles and albums sent to my desk every month from not only English Parlophone, Columbia, and HMV, but France, Germany, Italy, Japan, Austria, Australia, the Scandinavian countries and several other places, I am frankly amazed that we do not miss out on more hits as the months and years go by."

In May 1964, in a memo of his own, Livingston responded to Dexter's concerns (and the company's tentative initial treatment of the Beatles) by setting up a special committee to review the work of "EMI pop artists", writing that "the delicacy and risks of the acceptance or rejection of EMI pop artists by Capitol at the moment is such that I do not feel this obligation to accept or reject should fall on any one head".

In so doing, Livingston set up a "system whereby, in effect, the pop A&R department reviews every artist submitted which falls into a general pop vein". In short, Livingston was working to insulate Capitol Records as much as possible from unnecessarily angering its parent company.

Subsequently asked by Livingston to write a detailed report about the records that he had passed on during the previous year, specifically the Beatles, Dexter wrote back in October 1964: "in a carton containing 17 other singles, I received 'Love Me Do' and 'P.S. I Love You,' was not impressed, and so informed Tony Palmer [Dexter's EMI counterpart] by checking a 6 x 4 form and airmailing it back to him that same day. I have the carbon of this rejection

Opposite: Paul McCartney explains how it all works to American TV host Ed Sullivan.

Below: Another packed house in another US city as the Beatles conquered America.

along with the 17 other carbons as a museum piece which I will attach to this report."

As he notes in the memo, Dexter changed his tune in late summer, writing that "by the time I returned from England in August of 1963, it was apparent that the Beatles were the hottest thing England had ever encountered and when I learned that Swan had waived on the group, I then somewhat hysterically started urging Livingston, Gilmore and Dunn to exert every possible pressure on EMI and Epstein. Mainly, promises of a promotional campaign". At the conclusion of his memo, Dexter notes Beatles sales of more than 3.5 million records, outpacing any other Capitol artists by an incredible margin.

Over the next several years, Dexter exerted considerable influence upon the Beatles' American releases. Amazingly, despite personally neglecting to capitalize on the band's commercial possibilities throughout 1963, he was now responsible for overseeing their US promotion.

Released in April 1964, *The Beatles' Second Album*, for example, is noteworthy for additional echo and reverb effects intentionally added to the mix by Dexter, who wanted to give the album a "live" feel. He also believed that heavy doses of reverb rendered the Beatles more palatable for the American marketplace. At the same time, he rejected both the cover art and the track listings for the Beatles' original UK album releases, opting instead to revamp them for stateside consumption.

In August 1965, Livingston asked Dexter to account for the differences in the cover artwork between the UK and US releases, saying, "in a meeting with Brian Epstein yesterday, he expressed the very strong hope that we would consider using the same artwork for our Beatle album covers as England uses".

In his response, Dexter wrote, "No Capitol LP is ever identical *in repertoire* to the British LP ... Because EMI persists in the 14-track package we will *never* be in a position to release them simultaneously". He added, "We consider our artwork in virtually every case superior to the English front cover art, artistically as well as commercially. Ours is slanted more to the merchandising end; we also use more color than EMI ... Have you noticed that when Japan EMI, and numerous other affiliates, issue Beatles albums they more often than not use the Capitol front covers? ... Alan, if we have to wait around for British

covers in future it will compound our problems with Beatles product even more than now."

The very fact that Dexter perceived the existence of "problems with Beatles product" reveals an ironic mindset, given the remarkable sales records that the Fab Four were generating for Capitol. During the same period in which Dexter quibbled about replicating the Beatles' UK releases and cover art, he was significantly altering their sound, adding large amounts of reverb and echo to their 1964 and 1965 Capitol albums in order to Americanize their music. Dexter's efforts to alter the Beatles' overall sound are documented in the box sets *The Capitol Albums, Volume 1* (2004) and *Volume 2* (2006).

By 1966 Dexter had been demoted from his previously influential post as A&R representative. In the 1970s Dexter left Capitol altogether, eventually landing an editorial position with *Billboard* magazine. Following Lennon's assassination on December 8, 1980, Dexter became a flashpoint for the Beatles yet again, writing a notorious article in *Billboard* in which he criticized the recently fallen Beatle. The controversial piece, published 12 days after Lennon's murder, was entitled, "Nobody's Perfect: Lennon's Ego and Intransigence Irritated Those Who Knew Him".

In his scathing diatribe, Dexter wrote, "No pop artist since the early 1960s was more musically gifted than John Lennon. And of the four Beatles, Lennon was – among those in the industry who worked with him – the most disliked." Remarkably, Dexter goes on to recount Lennon and the Beatles' various failures, particularly the fact that they broke up when there were clearly many more financial bonanzas to be had by staying together.

Of his own role in manipulating the Beatles' sound stateside for Capitol, Dexter wrote, "When enough tapes arrived from England we spent hours adjusting the British Parlophone equalization and adding reverb to conform to Capitol's standards ... Lennon advised Capitol's management that he didn't care for the album covers Capitol was devising. Lennon didn't like the back covers, either. Nor did he approve of the sounds of the Beatles tapes issued by Capitol, an abrupt 180-degree turnaround from his previous praise ... McCartney, George Harrison, and Ringo Starr did not complain. Only Lennon."

Dexter concluded, "Lennon will be remembered well for his musical contributions. Unlike himself there was nothing eccentric or unlikable about John's artistry. And that's what all of us will remember." Not surprisingly, Dexter's tasteless article raised the ire of *Billboard*'s sponsors, forcing the magazine to publish a hasty apology for the article.

In subsequent years, Dexter rounded out his career with additional music journalism and production efforts, while never really shaking off his reputation as the man who gave the Beatles away. Dexter passed away from complications following a stroke in April 1990 at 74 years old. His impact on music is famously memorialized in Count Basie's "Diggin' for Dex", which is collected on *Basically Basie: Studio Dates, 1937-1945* (2006).

Yet as important as his contributions to the developing American jazz marketplace were, Dexter will always be remembered as the record executive who passed, time and time again, on the early opportunity to release the Beatles' music stateside.

As history has so resoundingly shown, he simply should've known better. His personal quest to derail the Beatles in 1963 and his later efforts to manipulate their sound and packaging resulted in a series of highly specific artefacts in the band's corpus.

Opposite: A ticket for the second of the Beatles' two 1964 shows at New York's Forest Hills Tennis Stadium.

Left: John Lennon during the Beatles' 1965 show at New York's Shea Stadium.

The American Beatles Albums

By 1967 and the much heralded release of *Sgt. Pepper's Lonely Hearts Club Band*, the Beatles' first seven UK albums – from *Please Please Me* through *Revolver* – had been repackaged by Capitol in the US as 11 separate recordings.

Before 1967, British Beatles fans had consumed dramatically different albums from their American counterparts. The hit song 'Yesterday', for example, originally appeared in England on *Help!*, while Capitol Records maximized the song's commercial appeal by using it as a vehicle for an American album release more than a year later on *Yesterday... and Today*.

Although the Beatles' UK record releases before 1967 featured an average of more than 45 minutes of music per album (or about 14 songs), their American recordings during that same era scarcely averaged more than 30 minutes (or about 10 songs).

Capitol scattered the contents of *Please Please Me*, which originally appeared in England in March 1963, across two different American album releases: *Meet the Beatles!* (1964) and *The Early Beatles* (1965). Capitol initially refused to release *Please Please Me* in America during the previous year when they considered the band to be merely a British act with little chance of stateside success.

The album took fewer than 14 hours to record and offers a fascinating glimpse into the first stages of their development as both songwriters and musicians. Marked by its tremendous energy and enthusiasm, *Please Please Me* also documents the beginning of the band's musical evolution at the hands of Martin.

In this way, Capitol's legitimate profit motives notwithstanding, the redistribution of the Beatles' first album undermines the seamless quality of *Please Please Me*'s musical continuity. In its original form, the album offers a quick study in the band's trademark combination of instrumental verve and lyrical balladry—from the staccato opening strains of 'I Saw Her Standing There' and the gentle romantic phrasings of 'Misery' and 'There's A Place' to 'Twist and Shout' and the album's raucous conclusion.

Ironically, despite their interest in furnishing incipient Beatles' fans with fresh product, Capitol's cannibalization of the album also resulted in the delay of their release of the album's title track by more than a year, when it finally surfaced on *The Early Beatles*. As Tim Riley notes in *Tell Me Why: A Beatles Commentary* (1988), such behavior amounted to "profiteering at its most corrupt".

When Dexter passed on the *Please Please Me* LP in early 1963, he also ironically succeeded in making the album's contents available for licensing to Vee-Jay, which released them as *Introducing the Beatles* in July 1963. Just six months later, Vee-Jay enjoyed unexpected profits when *Introducing the Beatles* became a runaway bestseller with the advent of the group's bravura appearance on *The Ed Sullivan Show*.

Capitol effectively exploited the swells of Beatlemania with a succession of additional album releases in 1964, parlaying the contents of the UK's *With The Beatles*, on to *Meet the Beatles!* and *The Beatles' Second Album* in America. Again, as with *Please Please Me*, Capitol's redistribution of *With The Beatles* diluted its place as a formative moment in their earlier musical canon.

Capitol's most egregious textual manipulation in the name of commerce occurred with the American release of *A Hard Day's Night*. While the band's third album appeared in England with 13 new songs in July 1964, Capitol redistributed five of the album's tracks on to the albums *Something New* and *Beatles '65* later that year. (Its title notwithstanding, *Beatles '65* first appeared in US record stores on December 15, 1964.)

The American release of *A Hard Day's Night* included eight of the UK record's tracks, in addition to four orchestral instrumentals from the film. Riley argues that the British version of the album "begins to show how the Beatles' music and the recording medium were meant for each other", a nuance of the record that would be lost on American audiences for years.

Capitol redeployed the contents of *Beatles For Sale*, the final UK album release from 1964, in order

Opposite: The Beatles cool off in the pool during their seven-day stay in Miami in February 1964.

to fill up the remaining space on *Something New* and *Beatles '65*. As 1964 came to a close, the Beatles' American distributor had already succeeded in reassembling three of their British albums into five hastily compiled American releases.

The degree to which Capitol altered their albums became apparent to the Beatles as they crisscrossed America on their endless stream of concert tours between 1964 and 1966. During their famous 1965 concert at Shea Stadium, for example, John Lennon erroneously introduced 'Baby's in Black' as a song from *Beatles VI*, when Capitol actually included the track on *Beatles '65*.

Later that year, the band came across the American version of *Help!* while travelling in California. A frustrated and angry Paul McCartney discovered that *Help!*, like *A Hard Day's Night* during the previous year, was released with a generous offering of soundtrack music and only seven of the songs that originally appeared on the UK album of the same name.

Years later, George Harrison still lamented the release of such "awful packages" during interviews. But while the band members bristled at the reassembly of their albums, Capitol's American marketing plan for the Beatles produced powerful economic results indeed. *Meet the Beatles!* sold 750,000 copies during its first week of release and by mid-March of 1964 had sold nearly four million units. Amazingly, fans purchased more than a million copies of *Beatles '65* in its first week of release during the 1964 Christmas rush.

Artistically, however, Capitol's redistribution of the tracks on *Rubber Soul* and *Revolver* constitutes an even greater affront to the listener interested in tracing the Beatles' musical and lyrical development. *Rubber Soul* continued the band's experimentation with new instruments and folk music that they began with *Help!*, while *Revolver* witnessed the emergence of psychedelia and the studio magic that would mark their greatest achievements during the latter half of the decade. Capitol repackaged the material on these two albums as three American releases – *Rubber Soul*, *Yesterday...and Today* and *Revolver*.

Set for release on June 20, 1966, *Yesterday...and Today* became the only Beatles album to actually *lose* money for Capitol Records. Just five days earlier, Capitol recalled 750,000 copies of the LP in a belated effort to replace its controversial cover

art. Known by Beatles fans and music critics alike as the "butcher" cover, Robert Whitaker's gory photograph featured the Beatles dressed in white laboratory coats, clutching decapitated baby dolls, and surrounded by raw meat.

Confronted by an avalanche of bad press, Capitol Records withdrew the cover artwork and released the album a few days later with a benign photograph of the group playfully posing around a steamer trunk. As it happened, Capitol ultimately failed to eradicate the offending cover. During the long weekend in which employees were busy removing *Yesterday ... and Today*'s cover artwork – at a reported cost of more than $200,000 – many fatigued workers resorted to merely pasting the new photograph over the "butcher" cover.

As a result, numerous fans discovered that they could carefully extricate the original photograph. The butcher cover has since become a much-desired item of Beatles memorabilia among serious collectors.

When it came to Capitol's repackaging of the band's work during this critical period in their artistic development, Riley astutely describes "this seeming innocent ploy for profits" as "drastically out of line with the Beatles' original intentions". He takes particular issue with the manner in which Capitol excised material from *Revolver*, effectively limiting Lennon's contribution to the album to a mere two tracks.

By so radically altering the context of the American *Revolver*, Capitol dramatically changed the nature of the Beatles' most significant moment of transition from the four fun-loving lads from Liverpool to the consummate studio craftsmen on such releases as *Sgt. Pepper*, *The Beatles* ("The White Album") and *Abbey Road*.

Although the Beatles never toured again after their final concert date at San Francisco's Candlestick Park in August 1966, they continued to produce albums together for more than three years. This lack of interest in promoting their product most likely explains the tighter control that they exerted on the American release of their albums after *Revolver*.

Nevertheless, Capitol succeeded in releasing two additional American compilations, *Magical Mystery Tour* (1967) and *Hey Jude* (1970), during the band's last years together. Ironically, the US release of *Magical Mystery Tour* has since emerged as the standard version of the album.

Left: Paul McCartney warms up backstage before another US concert in 1964.

Opposite: Paul McCartney and Ringo Starr under police protection in 1966.

In England, Parlophone released the album in an Extended Play format that was deleted after the global advent of the compact disc.

On the other hand, *Hey Jude* remains one of Capitol's most problematic repackaging efforts. Released nearly two years after its title track became an international hit, *Hey Jude* featured a haphazard selection of Beatles' material originally included on the flip sides of their recent singles. The album initially appeared under the unfortunate title of *The Beatles Again*, although it quickly soared to the upper regions of the album charts after being retitled.

After the Beatles disbanded in 1969, Capitol released a number of additional compilations in order to fulfil a recording contract that indebted the band to the record company through 1976. Of these albums, *Rock 'n' Roll Music* (1976) particularly underscores the ways in which Capitol carelessly sought to exploit their product.

Adorned with a cheeseburger and a portrait of Marilyn Monroe, *Rock 'n' Roll Music* inaccurately associates the band with an earlier era, a marketing gaffe of remarkable proportions. "All of us looked at the cover of *Rock 'n' Roll Music* and we could hardly bear to see it," Ringo Starr complained in the music press. "The cover was disgusting ... All that Coca-Cola and cars with big fins was the fifties."

Capitol's approach to much of the Beatles' prodigious musical corpus, especially evidenced by their cover design for *Rock 'n' Roll Music*, demonstrates how little the firm really knew about the artistic nature of their most commercially viable act.

The 1987 release of the Beatles' albums on compact disc led to the discontinuation of the American albums in favour of the British releases, save for the aforementioned retrospective releases of *The Capitol Albums* in the early twenty-first century. Until that time, the group's LPs held sway in US record stores for more than two decades, a period when – during those pre-Internet days – the vast majority of American Beatles fans understood the band's evolution in an incomplete and haphazard fashion.

While music critics resoundingly credit the Fab Four with changing the face of popular music, Ian MacDonald ruefully reminds us in *Revolution in the Head: The Beatles' Records and the Sixties* (1994) that the "only aspect of pop the Beatles failed to change was the business itself". Although they altered their industry in nearly every conceivable fashion, "they nevertheless ended their career together on the time-honoured killing-field of the contractual dispute. Twenty-five years after them, the commerce in this area continues to move in the traditional direction: into the bank accounts of the money men."

MacDonald's conclusion, and its implications for other icons of popular music and art forms that enjoy a wide audience, underscores the importance of preserving world culture's most cherished artefacts in adherence to their creators' original vision.

Below: The Beatles pose in front of the stars and bars of the US flag, 1964.

The Beatles' US Album Discography 1963–1970

Introducing the Beatles

Released July 22, 1963 (Vee-Jay)

I Saw Her Standing There, Misery, Anna (Go To Him), Chains, Boys, Love Me Do, P.S. I Love You, Baby It's You, Do You Want To Know A Secret, A Taste Of Honey, There's A Place, Twist And Shout.

Meet the Beatles!

Released January 20, 1964 (Capitol)

I Want To Hold Your Hand, I Saw Her Standing There, This Boy, It Won't Be Long, All I've Got To Do, All My Loving, Don't Bother Me, Little Child, Till There Was You, Hold Me Tight, I Wanna Be Your Man, Not A Second Time.

The Beatles' Second Album

Released April 10, 1964 (Capitol)

Roll Over Beethoven, Thank You Girl, You Really Got A Hold On Me, Devil In Her Heart, Money, You Can't Do That, Long Tall Sally, I Call Your Name, Please Mister Postman, I'll Get You, She Loves You.

A Hard Day's Night

Released June 26, 1964 (United Artists)

A Hard Day's Night, Tell Me Why, I'll Cry Instead, I Should Have Known Better (instrumental), I'm Happy Just To Dance, And I Love Her (instrumental), I Should Have Known Better, If I Fell, Ringo's Theme (This Boy), Can't Buy Me Love, A Hard Day's Night Instrumental).

Something New

Released July 20, 1964 (Capitol)

I'll Cry Instead, Things We Said Today, Any Time At All, When I Get Home, Slow Down, Matchbox, Tell Me Why, And I Love Her, I'm Happy Just To Dance With You, If I Fell, Komm, Gib Mir Deine Hand.

Beatles '65

Released December 15, 1964 (Capitol)

No Reply, I'm A Loser, Baby's In Black, Rock And Roll Music, I'll Follow The Sun, Mr. Moonlight, Honey Don't, I'll Be Back, She's a Woman, I Feel Fine, Everybody's Trying To Be My Baby.

The Early Beatles

Released March 22, 1965 (Capitol)

Love Me Do, Twist And Shout, Anna (Go To Him), Chains, Boys, Ask Me Why, Please Please Me, P.S. I Love You, Baby It's You, A Taste Of Honey, Do You Want To Know A Secret.

Beatles V1

Released June 14, 1965 (Capitol)

Kansas City/Hey Hey Hey Hey, Eight Days A Week, You Like Me Too Much, Bad Bay, I Don't Want To Spoil Your Party, Words Of Love, What You're Doing, Yes It Is, Dizzy Miss Lizzy, Tell Me What You See, Every Little Thing.

Help!

Released August 13, 1965 (Capitol)

Help!, The Night Before, You've Got To Hide Your Love Away, I Need You, Another Girl, You're Gonna Lost That Girl, Ticket To Ride, The Bitter End, Another Hard Day's Night, The Chase, From Me To You Fantasy, In The Tyrol.

Rubber Soul

Released December 6, 1965 (Capitol)

I've Just Seen A Face, Norwegian Wood (This Bird Has Flown), You Won't See Me, Think For Yourself, The Word, Michelle, It's Only Love, I'm Looking Through You, In My Life, Wait, Run For Your Life.

Yesterday . . . and Today

Released June 20, 1966 (Capitol)

Drive My Car, I'm Only Sleeping, Nowhere Man, Doctor Robert, Yesterday, Act Naturally, And Your Bird Can Sing, If I Needed Someone, We Can Work it Out, What Goes On, Day Tripper.

Revolver

Released August 8, 1966 (Capitol)

Taxman, Eleanor Rigby, Love You to, Here There And Everywhere, Yellow Submarine, She Said She Said, Good Day Sunshine, For No One, I Want To Tell You, Got To Get You Into My Life, Tomorrow Never Knows.

Sgt. Pepper's Lonely Hearts Club Band

Released June 2, 1967 (Capitol)

Sgt. Pepper's Lonely Hearts Club Band, With A Little Help From My Friends, Lucy in the Sky With Diamonds, Getting Better, Fixing A Hole, She's Leaving Home, Being For The Benefit Of Mr. Kite, Within You Without You, When I'm Sixty Four, Lovely Rita, Good Morning Good Morning, Sgt. Pepper's Lonely Hearts Club Band (Reprise), A Day In the Life.

Magical Mystery Tour

Released November 27, 1967 (Capitol)

Magical Mystery Tour, The Fool On the Hill, Flying, Blue Jay Way, Your Mother Should Know, I Am The Walrus, Hello Goodbye, Strawberry Fields Forever, Penny Lane, Baby You're A Rich Man, All You Need Is Love.

The Beatles

Released November 25, 1968 (Apple/Capitol)

Back In The USSR, Dear Prudence, Glass Onion, Ob-La-Di Ob-La-Da, Wild Honey Pie, The Continuing Story Of Bungalow Bill, While My Guitar Gently Weeps, Happiness Is A Warm Gun, Martha My Dear, I'm So Tired, Blackbird, Piggies, Rocky Raccoon, Don't Pass Me By, Why Don't We Do It In The Road, I Will, Julia, Birthday, Yer Blues, Mother Nature's Son, Everybody's Got Something To Hide Except Me And My Monkey, Sexy Sadie, Helter Skelter, Long Long Long, Revolution 1, Honey Pie, Savoy Truffle, Cry Baby Cry, Revolution 9, Good Night.

Yellow Submarine

Released January 13, 1969 (Apple/Capitol)

Yellow Submarine, Only A Northern Song, All Together Now, Hey Bulldog, It's All Too Much, All You Need Is Love, Pepperland, Sea Of Time, Sea Of Holes, Sea Of Monsters, March Of The Meanies, Pepperland Laid Waste, Yellow Submarine In Pepperland.

Abbey Road

Released October 1, 1969 (Apple/Capitol)

Come Together, Something, Maxwell's Silver Hammer, Oh! Darling, Octopus's Garden, I Want You (She's So Heavy), Here Comes The Sun, Because, You Never Give Me Your Money, Sun King, Mean Mr Mustard, Polythene Pam, She Came In The Bathroom Window, Golden Slumbers, Carry That Weight, The End, Her Majesty.

Hey Jude

Released February 26, 1970 (Apple/Capitol)

Can't Buy Me Love, I Should Have Known Better, Paperback Writer, Rain, Lady Madonna, Revolution, Hey Jude, Old Brown Shoe, Don't Let Me Down, The Ballad Of John And Yoko.

Let It Be

Released May 18, 1970 (Apple/Capitol)

Two Of Us, Dig A Pony, Across the Universe, I Me Mine, Dig It, Let It Be, Maggie Mae, I've Got A Feeling, The One After 909, The Long And Winding Road, For You Blue, Get Back.

Left: 25,000 fans saw the Beatles when they played at a horse racing course in Massachusetts in 1966.

Opposite: The Beatles were greeted by 9,000 fans when they arrived at San Francisco airport on the eve of their final concert.

- Bruce Springsteen, in his autobiography *Born to Run,* wrote, "*The* album cover, the greatest album cover of all time (tied with *Highway 61 Revisited*). All it said was "Meet the Beatles". That was exactly what I wanted to do. Those four half-shadowed faces – rock 'n' roll's Mount Rushmore – and the HAIR! The HAIR! What did it mean? It was a surprise, a shock. You couldn't see them on the radio. I didn't want to *meet* the Beatles, I wanted to BE the Beatles."

- Roger McGuinn of the Byrds told *Modern Guitars* magazine, "Early on, the Byrds went to see *A Hard Day's Night*, a kind of reconnaissance trip. And we took notes on what the Beatles were playing and bought instruments like they had. I got really jazzed by the Beatles. I loved what they were doing."

- The Beach Boys' Brian Wilson wrote in his autobiography *I Am Brian Wilson,* "The one that really got me was *Rubber Soul*, which came out at the end of 1965. *Rubber Soul* is probably the greatest record ever. It's a whole album of Beatles folk songs, a whole album where everything flows together and everything works.
    I tried *Pet Sounds* as an answer to *Rubber Soul* and I understood that Paul McCartney really liked that sound and then they went into the studio and did *Sgt. Pepper*. Damn! They exploded into creativity. It was a competitive thing but they were in a world of their own."

- In his autobiography *Good Vibrations,* Beach Boy Mike Love wrote, "We listened to the US version of the Beatles' *Rubber Soul* album, which discarded past conventions – one or two hit songs, the rest fillers – and presented a unified musical narrative or, as Brian said, 'A whole album with all good stuff'."

- Joni Mitchell, speaking with *Rockcellar* magazine, said, "*Rubber Soul* was the Beatle album I played over and over. I think they were discovering Dylan and the songs often had an acoustic feel. The whole scenario has this whimsical, charmingly wry quality with a bit of dark undertone."

Chronology

1940

July 7
Richard Starkey is born in Liverpool. He later changes his name to Ringo Starr.

October 9
John Lennon is born in Liverpool.

1942

June 18
Paul McCartney is born in Liverpool.

1943

February 24
George Harrison is born in Liverpool.

1956

Summer
Aged 16, John Lennon forms a band called the Quarrymen, with some friends from Quarry Bank Grammar School.

1957

July 6
The Quarrymen perform at St Peter's Woolton Parish Church. Afterwards, John Lennon meets Paul McCartney. McCartney is 15 at the time. Soon after this first meeting, John asks Paul to join the Quarrymen.

1958

February
George Harrison joins the Quarrymen. He is 15 years old.

1960

January
Stuart Sutcliffe, John Lennon's friend from the Liverpool College of Art, joins the Quarrymen. They bcome the Silver Beetles and later the Silver Beatles.

August
Pete Best joins the band as their drummer. The group has once again changed its name, this time to the Beatles. The group travels to Hamburg in Germany for the first of five trips there between August 1960 and December 1962. In Hamburg, they perform at clubs such as the *Kaiserkeller* and *Indra*.

December 27
Returning to Liverpool from Hamburg, the Beatles play Litherland Town Hall. The performance creates genuine excitement in the area.

1961

Spring
Stuart Sutcliffe leaves the band.

November
The Beatles meet Brian Epstein. He becomes their manager.

1962

January 1
The band has an unsuccessful audition with Decca Records in London.

April 10
Stuart Sutcliffe dies from a brain haemorrhage.

May 9
The band sign their first recording contract. They hire George Martin to be their producer.

August 16
Pete Best leaves the band.

August 18
Ringo Starr joins the Beatles.

September 11
The Beatles record their first single, 'Love Me Do'.

October 5
'Love Me Do' is released in the United Kingdom. It peaks at number 17 on the British chart.

1963

January 11
The Beatles' second single, 'Please Please Me', is released in the United Kingdom.

February 11
The Beatles record their first album, *Please Please Me*, in one day.

February 22
The song 'Please Please Me' hits number one on the British singles chart and remains there for two weeks.

March 22
The album *Please Please Me* is released in the UK and is an instant hit. The album is number one for 29 weeks.

July
The album *Please Please Me* is released in the United States, but is titled *Introducing the Beatles*. The release is a flop.

October
The Beatles' popularity spreads from the UK throughout Europe. 'Beatlemania' begins.

October 13
15 million people watch the Beatles perform on ITV's *Sunday Night at the London Palladium*.

November 4
The Beatles perform for Queen Elizabeth II, Princess Margaret and Lord Snowdon at the Royal Command Performance. During the performance, Lennon famously shouts out, 'Will the people in the cheaper seats clap their hands? And the rest of you, if you'll just rattle your jewellery.'

November 22
With the Beatles – the Beatles' second album – is released in the UK exactly eight months after their debut album. It holds the number one position on the British album chart for 21 weeks, knocking the Beatles' own first album off number one. The two albums combine to dominate the top of the album charts for 51 straight weeks.

November 29
'I Want To Hold Your Hand' is released in the UK and goes straight to the top of the charts.

December 26
'I Want To Hold Your Hand' is released in the US and goes to number one, where it remains for seven weeks.

1964

January 20
Capitol Records releases *Meet the Beatles!* in the United States.

February 7
The 'British Invasion' begins when the Beatles land at JFK Airport in New York.

February 9
A record 73 million people watch the Beatles on *The Ed Sullivan Show*.

February 11
The Beatles perform live at the Washington Coliseum in Washington D.C., their first performance in the United States.

12 February
The Beatles perform live in New York City for the first time. The concert is staged at Carnegie Hall.

February 15
Meet the Beatles! reaches the number one spot on *Billboard*'s US album chart. It stays there for 11 weeks.

March 2
The Beatles begin making their first film, A *Hard Day's Night*. Filming is completed in eight weeks.

March 31
The Beatles have songs in the top five positions of the *Billboard*'s singles chart at the same time. This is a first for *Billboard*. The songs, in order of their charting position, are: 'Can't Buy Me Love', 'Twist and Shout', 'She Loves You', 'I Want To Hold Your Hand' and 'Please Please Me'.

April 4
The Beatles have 14 songs in *Billboard*'s Hot 100 singles chart.

July 6
A Hard Day's Night premieres in London and receives good reviews from both the public and critics.

July 10
The soundtrack of *A Hard Day's Night* is released in the UK, where it immediately hits number one on the British album chart.

August 11
The film *A Hard Day's Night* opens in the US and becomes an instant hit.

August
The soundtrack of *A Hard Day's Night* is released in the US and goes straight to number one.

August 19
The Beatles begin their tour of the US and Canada in San Francisco at the Cow Palace. The tour lasts one month.

December 4
The album *Beatles For Sale* comes out in the UK and instantly takes the number one spot on the British albums chart.

1965
February 23
The Beatles begin shooting their second movie, *Help!*. Filming takes place in the Bahamas.

June 12
The Queen names the Beatles Members of the British Empire.

July 29
Help! has its London premiere. The film is a hit.

August 6
The album *Help!* is released in the UK and becomes number one on the British album chart.

August 11
The film *Help!* opens in the United States, where it is also a hit.

August 15
The Beatles perform at Shea Stadium in New York for 55,600 people, a record figure for concert attendance at the time.

December 3
Rubber Soul is released in the UK and goes straight to number one on the British album chart. The album

is released three days later in the US and spends six weeks at the top of the *Billboard* album chart.

1966
August 5
Revolver is released in the UK and goes straight to number one on the British album chart.

August 29
The Beatles perform their last live concert in San Francisco, California.

1967
June 1
Sgt. Pepper's Lonely Hearts Club Band is released in the UK and goes straight to the number one spot on Britain's album chart, where it remains for 27 weeks.

June 25
Our World, a two-hour television programme about the Beatles, airs in 24 countries via satellite. It is the first live television show ever to air worldwide.

August 27
Upon learning that their manager, Brian Epstein, has died, the Beatles visit Maharishi Mahesh Yogi in Bangor, north Wales, to learn about Transcendental Meditation.

November 27
Magical Mystery Tour is released in the US and goes to number one on *Billboard*'s album chart.

December 26
The hour-long special *Magical Mystery Tour*, featuring the Beatles, airs in the UK and is panned by critics. Nevertheless, it is watched by an estimated 14 million people.

1968
February
The Beatles spend several weeks in Rishikesh, India, where they attend a seminar by Maharishi Mahesh Yogi on Transcendental Meditation.

May 14
John Lennon and Paul McCartney guest on *The Tonight Show* and announce their new company, Apple (Apple Corps Ltd), designed to help young artists.

July 17
The animated film *Yellow Submarine* premieres in London.

November 22
The album *The Beatles* is released in Britain and the United States. It goes straight to number one in both countries. The album is also known as *The White Album*.

1969
January 13
The soundtrack of *Yellow Submarine* is released in the US and reaches the number two position on *Billboard*'s album chart. *The White Album* is simultaneously in the number one position.

January 30
The Beatles perform together for the very last time on the rooftop of Apple Corps Ltd at Savile Row in London.

September
John Lennon decides to leave the Beatles, although he does not announce his decision publicly due to contract negotiations with the label EMI.

September 26
Abbey Road is released in the UK, where it goes straight to the top of the charts. It is the Beatles' last studio album.

November 25
John Lennon returns his Member of the British Empire medal as an anti-war protest.

1970
11 January
Paul McCartney announces that he has left the Beatles.

May 8
The album *Let It Be*, which was actually recorded before *Abbey Road*, is released in the UK. It shoots straight to the top of the British album chart.

May 20
The documentary *Let It Be* premieres in London. None of the Beatles are in attendance at the showing.

1980
December 8
John Lennon is shot and killed in New York City.

2001
November 29
George Harrison dies of cancer in Los Angeles.

2010
November 16
The Beatles' entire music catalogue is released on iTunes.

Discography

The Beatles' UK Album Discography 1963–1970

Please Please Me
Released March 22, 1963 (Parlophone)
I Saw Her Standing There, Misery, Anna (Go To Him), Chains, Boys, Ask Me Why, Please Please Me, Love Me Do, PS I Love You, Baby It's You, Do You Want To Know A Secret, A Taste Of Honey, There's a Place Twist and Shout.

With The Beatles
Released November 22, 1963 (Parlophone)
It Won't Be Long, All I've Got To Do, All My Loving, Don't Bother Me, Little Child, Till There Was You, Please Mister Postman, Roll Over Beethoven, Hold Me Tight, You Really Got A Hold On Me, I Wanna Be Your Man, Devil In Her Heart, Not A Second Time, Money (That's What I Want).

A Hard Day's Night
Released July 10, 1964 (Parlophone)
A Hard Day's Night, I Should Have Known Better, If I Fell, I'm Happy Just To Dance With You, And I Love Her, Tell Me Why, Can't Buy Me Love, Any Time At All, I'll Cry Instead, Things We Said Today, When I Get Home, You Can't Do That, I'll Be Back.

Beatles For Sale
Released December 4, 1964 (Parlophone)
No Reply, I'm A Loser, Baby's In Black, Rock And Roll Music, I'll Follow The Sun, Mr Moonlight, Kansas City/Hey-Hey-Hey-Hey!, Eight Days A Week, Words Of Love, Honey Don't, Every Little Thing, I Don't Want To Spoil The Party, What You're Doing, Everybody's Trying To Be My Baby.

Help!
Released August 6, 1965 (Parlophone)
Help!, The Night Before, You've Got To Hide Your Love Away, I Need You, Another Girl, You're Going To Lose That Girl, Ticket To Ride, Act Naturally, It's Only Love, You Like Me Too Much, Tell Me What You See, I've Just Seen A Face, Yesterday, Dizzy Miss Lizzy.

Rubber Soul
Released December 3, 1965 (Parlophone)
Drive My Car, Norwegian Wood (This Bird Has Flown), You Won't See Me, Nowhere Man, Think For Yourself, The Word, Michelle, What Goes On, Girl, I'm Looking Through You, In My Life, Wait, If I Needed Someone, Run For Your Life.

Revolver
Released August 5, 1966 (Parlophone)
Taxman, Eleanor Rigby, I'm Only Sleeping, Love You To, Here, There And Everywhere, Yellow Submarine, She Said She Said, Good Day Sunshine, And Your Bird Can Sing, For No One, Doctor Robert, I Want To Tell You, Got To Get You Into My Life, Tomorrow Never Knows.

A Collection Of Beatles Oldies
Released December 9, 1966 (Parlophone)
She Loves You, From Me to You, We Can Work It Out, Help!, Michelle, Yesterday, I Feel Fine, Yellow Submarine, Can't Buy Me Love, Bad Boy, Day Tripper, A Hard Day's Night, Ticket To Ride, Paperback Writer, Eleanor Rigby, I Want To Hold Your Hand.

Sgt Pepper's Lonely Hearts Club Band
Released June 1, 1967 (Parlophone)
Sgt Pepper's Lonely Hearts Club Band, With A Little Help From My Friends, Lucy In The Sky With Diamonds, Getting Better, Fixing A Hole, She's Leaving Home, Being For The Benefit Of Mr Kite!, Within You Without You, When I'm Sixty-Four, Lovely Rita, Good Morning Good Morning, Sgt Pepper's Lonely Hearts Club Band (Reprise), A Day In The Life.

The Beatles (White Album)
Released November 22, 1968 (Apple)
Back In The USSR, Dear Prudence, Glass Onion, Ob-La-Di, Ob-La-Da, Wild Honey Pie, The Continuing Story Of Bungalow Bill, While My Guitar Gently Weeps, Happiness Is A Warm Gun, Martha My Dear, I'm So Tired, Blackbird, Piggies, Rocky Raccoon, Don't Pass Me By, Why Don't We Do It In The Road?, I Will, Julia, Birthday, Yer Blues, Mother Nature's Son, Everybody's Got Something To Hide Except Me And My Monkey, Sexy Sadie, Helter Skelter, Long, Long, Long, Revolution 1, Honey Pie, Savoy Truffle, Cry Baby Cry, Revolution 9 Good Night.

Yellow Submarine
Released January 17, 1969 (Apple/Parlophone)
Yellow Submarine, Only A Northern Song, All Together Now, Hey Bulldog, It's All Too Much, All You Need Is Love, Pepperland, Sea Of Time, Sea Of Holes, Sea Of Monsters, March Of The Meanies, Pepperland Laid Waste, Yellow Submarine In Pepperland.

Abbey Road
Released September 26, 1969 (Apple)
Come Together, Something, Maxwell's Silver Hammer, Oh! Darling, Octopus's Garden, I Want You (She's So Heavy), Here Comes The Sun, Because, You Never Give Me Your Money, Sun King, Mean Mr Mustard, Polythene Pam, She Came In Through The Bathroom Window, Golden Slumbers, Carry That Weight, The End, Her Majesty.

Let It Be
Released May 8, 1970 (Apple)
Two Of Us, Dig A Pony, Across The Universe, I Me Mine, Dig It, Let It Be, Maggie Mae, I've Got A Feeling, One After 909, The Long And Winding Road, For You Blue, Get Back.

The Beatles' US Album Discography 1963–1970

Introducing the Beatles
Released July 22, 1963 (Vee-Jay)
I Saw Her Standing There, Misery,Anna (Go To Him), Chains, Boys, Love Me Do, P.S. I Love You, Baby It's You, Do You Want To Know A Secret, A Taste Of Honey, There's A Place, Twist And Shout.

Meet the Beatles!
Released January 20, 1964 (Capitol)
I Want To Hold Your Hand, I Saw Her Standing There, This Boy, It Won't Be Long, All I've Got To Do, All My Loving, Don't Bother Me, Little Child, Till There Was You, Hold Me Tight, I Wanna Be Your Man, Not A Second Time.

The Beatles' Second Album
Released April 10, 1964 (Capitol)
Roll Over Beethoven, Thank You Girl, You Really Got A Hold On Me, Devil In Her Heart, Money, You Can't Do That, Long Tall Sally, I Call Your Name, Please Mister Postman, I'll Get You, She Loves You.

A Hard Day's Night
Released June 26, 1964 (United Artists)
A Hard Day's Night, Tell Me Why, I'll Cry Instead, I Should Have Known Better (instrumental), I'm Happy Just To Dance, And I Love Her (instrumental), I Should Have Known Better, If I Fell, Ringo's Theme (This Boy), Can't Buy Me Love, A Hard Day's Night Instrumental).

Something New
Released July 20, 1964 (Capitol)
I'll Cry Instead, Things We Said Today, Any Time At All, When I Get Home, Slow Down, Matchbox, Tell Me Why, And I Love Her, I'm Happy Just To Dance With You, If I Fell, Komm, Gib Mir Deine Hand.

Beatles '65
Released December 15, 1964 (Capitol)
No Reply, I'm A Loser, Baby's In Black, Rock And Roll Music, I'll Follow The Sun, Mr. Moonlight, Honey Don't, I'll Be Back, She's a Woman, I Feel Fine, Everybody's Trying To Be My Baby.

The Early Beatles
Released March 22, 1965 (Capitol)
Love Me Do, Twist And Shout, Anna (Go To Him), Chains, Boys, Ask Me Why, Please Please Me, P.S. I Love You, Baby It's You, A Taste Of Honey, Do You Want To Know A Secret.

Beatles V1
Released June 14, 1965 (Capitol)
Kansas City/Hey Hey Hey Hey, Eight Days A Week, You Like Me Too Much, Bad Bay, I Don't Want To Spoil Your Party, Words Of Love, What You're Doing, Yes It Is, Dizzy Miss Lizzy, Tell Me What You See, Every Little Thing.

Help!
Released August 13, 1965 (Capitol)
Help!, The Night Before, You've Got To Hide Your Love Away, I Need You, Another Girl, You're Gonna Lost That Girl, Ticket To Ride, The Bitter End, Another Hard Day's Night, The Chase, From Me To You Fantasy, In The Tyrol.

Rubber Soul
Released December 6, 1965 (Capitol)
I've Just Seen A Face, Norwegian Wood (This Bird Has Flown), You Won't See Me, Think For Yourself, The Word, Michelle, It's Only Love, I'm Looking Through You, In My Life, Wait, Run For Your Life.

Yesterday . . . and Today
Released June 20, 1966 (Capitol)
Drive My Car, I'm Only Sleeping, Nowhere Man, Doctor Robert, Yesterday, Act Naturally, And Your Bird Can Sing, If I Needed Someone, We Can Work it Out, What Goes On, Day Tripper.

Revolver
Released August 8, 1966 (Capitol)
Taxman, Eleanor Rigby, Love You to, Here There And Everywhere, Yellow Submarine, She Said She Said, Good Day Sunshine, For No One, I Want To Tell You, Got To Get You Into My Life, Tomorrow Never Knows.

Sgt. Pepper's Lonely Hearts Club Band
Released June 2, 1967 (Capitol)
Sgt. Pepper's Lonely Hearts Club Band, With A Little Help From My Friends, Lucy in the Sky With Diamonds, Getting Better, Fixing A Hole, She's Leaving Home, Being For The Benefit Of Mr. Kite, Within You Without You, When I'm Sixty Four, Lovely Rita, Good Morning Good Morning, Sgt. Pepper's Lonely Hearts Club Band (Reprise), A Day Inthe Life.

Magical Mystery Tour
Released November 27, 1967 (Capitol)
Magical Mystery Tour, The Fool On the Hill, Flying, Blue Jay Way, Your Mother Should Know, I Am The Walrus, Hello Goodbye, Strawberry Fields Forever,Penny Lane, Baby You're A Rich Man, All You Need Is Love.

The Beatles
Released November 25, 1968 (Apple/Capitol)
Back In The USSR, Dear Prudence, Glass Onion, Ob-La-Di Ob-La-Da, Wild Honey Pie, The Continuing Story Of Bungalow Bill, While My Guitar Gently Weeps, Happiness Is A Warm Gun, Martha My Dear, I'm So Tired, Blackbird, Piggies, Rocky Raccoon, Don't Pass Me By, Why Don't We Do It In The Road, I Will, Julia, Birthday, Yer Blues, Mother Nature's Son, Everybody's Got Something To Hide Except Me And My Monkey, Sexy Sadie, Helter Skelter, Long Long Long, Revolution 1, Honey Pie, Savoy Truffle, Cry Baby Cry, Revolution 9, Good Night.

Yellow Submarine
Released January 13, 1969 (Apple/Capitol)
Yellow Submarine, Only A Northern Song, All Together Now, Hey Bulldog, It's All Too Much, All You Need Is Love, Pepperland, Sea Of Time, Sea Of Holes, Sea Of Monsters, March Of The Meanies, Pepperland Laid Waste, Yellow Submarine In Pepperland.

Abbey Road
Released October 1, 1969 (Apple/Capitol)
Come Together, Something, Maxwell's Silver Hammer, Oh! Darling, Octopus's Garden, I Want You (She's So Heavy), Here Comes The Sun, Because, You Never Give Me Your Money, Sun King, Mean Mr Mustard, Polythene Pam, She Came In The Bathroom Window, Golden Slumbers, Carry That Weight, The End, Her Majesty.

Hey Jude
Released February 26, 1970 (Apple/Capitol)
Can't Buy Me Love, I Should Have Known Better, Paperback Writer, Rain, Lady Madonna, Revolution, Hey Jude, Old Brown Shoe, Don't Let Me Down, The Ballad Of John And Yoko.

Let It Be
Released May 18, 1970 (Apple/Capitol)
Two Of Us, Dig A Pony, Across the Universe, I Me Mine, Dig It, Let It Be, Maggie Mae, I've Got A Feeling, The One After 909, The Long And Winding Road, For You Blue, Get Back.

Acknowledgements

Thanks, as ever, go to Roland Hall at Carlton Books for his enthusiasm and support and to all the people at Carlton who helped in the creation of this book. Also, obviously to all those who gave up their time to share stories and memories of their favourite Beatles albums with me – there wouldn't be a book without you – so thanks again.

Finally, thanks to the British Library for being there with their comprehensive collection of back issues including *Billboard* magazine, *Melody Maker*, *Music Week*, *New Musical Express*, *Record Retailer*, *Crawdaddy*, *Rolling Stone* and Q magazine, plus assorted national newspapers. I am also grateful to the Beatles Bible website (www.beatlesbible.com).

Bibliography

Tony Barrow, *John, Paul, George, Ringo & Me* (Andre Deutsch 2006)

Beatles in Their Own Words, compiled by Miles (Omnibus Press 1978)

The Beatles, The Beatles Anthology (Cassell & Co 2000)

Peter Brown and Steven Gaines, *The Love You Make: An Insider's Story of the Beatles* (McGraw-Hill 1983)

Tony Bramwell with Rosemary Kingsland, *Magical Mystery Tours: My Life With the Beatles* (Robson Books 2005)

Ray Coleman, *Lennon: The Definitive Biography* (Pan 1995)

Geoff Emerick, *Here, There and Everywhere: My Life Recording the Music of the Beatles* (Gotham Books 2006)

Bill Harry, *The Beatles Encyclopedia* (Virgin Books 2000)

Mark Lewisohn, *The Complete Beatles Recording Sessions* (Hamlyn 1988)

Mike Love, *Good Vibrations* (Faber & Faber 2016)

George Martin *All You Need Is Ears* (St Martin's Press 1979)

Graham Nash, *Wild Tales* (Penguin 2014)

Craig Rosen, *Billboard Book of Number One Albums: the Inside Story Behind Pop Music's Blockbuster Records* (Billboard Books 1996)

Brian Southall, *Abbey Road* (Patrick Stephens 1982)

Bruce Springsteen *Born To Run* (Simon & Schuster 2017)

Brian Wilson *I Am Brian Wilson: The Genius Behind the Beach Boys* (Coronet 2016)

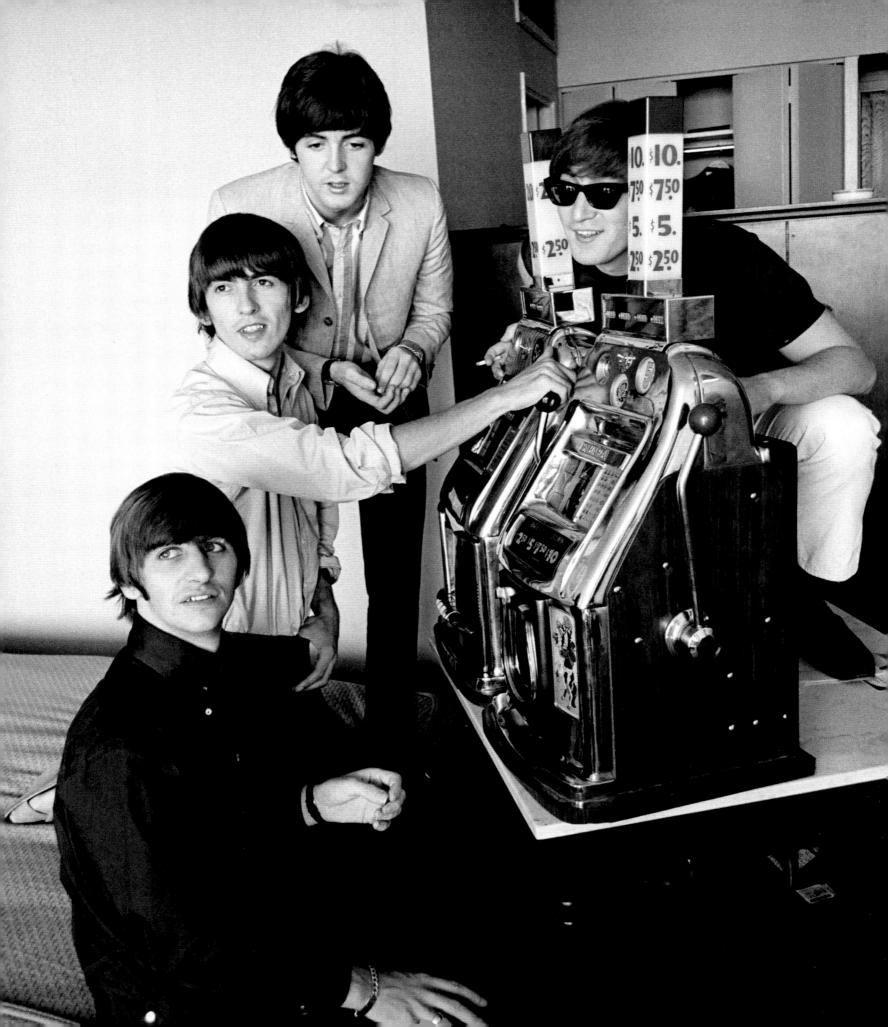

Index

Index of Songs

Credits

The publishers would like to thank the following sources for their kind permission to reproduce the pictures in this book.

Key: t = top, b = bottom, c = centre, l = left & r = right

Alamy: Marka 196-197; /ZUMA Press, Inc.: 201

Camera Press, London: Photograph by Tom Murray 198, 213

Getty Images: Fiona Adams/Redferns 33; /Alert/ullstein bild 153b; /Ambor/ullstein bild 144-145; /Harry Benson/Express 74-75, 86-87, 154-155, 299; /Bentley Archive/Popperfoto 211, 237b; /Bettmann 16-17, 130t, 142, 194, 216, 229, 258, 269; /Ted Blackbrow/Daily Mail 265b; /John Bulmer 247; /Leonard Burt/Central Press 265t; /Cattani/Daily Mail 195r; /Central Press 20-21, 66-67, 186; /Christies 234; /Archivio Cicconi 24; /Cummings Archives/Redferns 138, 182-183, 192, 230, 263; /John Downing 164, 174; /Larry Ellis/Express 166-167, 199; /Tony Evans/Timelapse Library Ltd. 204; /Express 232-233; /Express/Archive Photos 92-93, 110-111; /Fox Photos 34, 63, 75; /GAB Archives 35, 279; /Ron Galella/Ron Galella Collection 271; /Jim Gray/Keystone/Hulton Archive 71b, 165b; /Harry Hammond/V&A Images 13; /Koh Hasebe/Shinko Music 127, 165t, 171t, 188, 278-279; /Mark and Colleen Hayward/Redferns 25, 69, 78tl, 78bl, 125, 179, 184, 225; /Frank H. Hill/The Boston Globe 277; /Jeff Hochberg 218-219, 274, 283, 292; /Jim Hughes/NY Daily News Archive 119t; /Hulton-Archive 160-161; /Hulton-Deutsch Collection/Corbis 109, 223; /Imagno 103r; /Keystone 107l, 240; /Keystone/Hulton Archive 169, 185, 187, 244-245, 249; /K & K Ulf Kruger OHG/Redferns 32; /Robert Landau/Corbis 226-227; /Les Lee/Express 104b; /LMPC 214-215; /John Loengard/Life Magazine/The LIFE Picture Collection 287; /William Lovelace/Express 26-27, 78r, 282; /David Magnus 52; / C. Maher/Daily Express/Hulton Archive 200, 221, 224, 248, 250-251; /Andrew Maclear/Redferns 235, 252-253; /Stan Meagher/Express 100; /Michael Ochs Archive 73t, 88b, 94-95, 98-99, 117, 162, 180, 260b, 261, 290; /Movie Poster Image Art 207; /Terry O'Neill/Iconic Images 28, 30-31, 40-41, 128; /© Norman Parkinson Achive/Iconic Images 64-65; /Jan Persson/Redferns 231, 239; /Popperfoto 37, 38, 59, 60-61, 70, 242-243, 256, 257, 275, 289; /Paul Popper/Popperfoto 276; /Potter/Express/Hulton Archive 177; /John Pratt/Keystone 176; /Pierluigi Praturlon 130b; /Michael Putland 202t; /Bill Ray/The LIFE Picture Collection 84t, 293; /David Redfern/Redferns 36, 48, 172, 173, 175; /Rolls Press/Popperfoto 72, 77, 82-83, 85, 102, 104t, 120-121, 163, 170, 189; /Max Scheler - K & K/Redferns 73b; /Chris Smith/Popperfoto 80; /SSPL 246; /George Stroud/Express/Hulton Archive 10-11, 147; / Len Trievnor/Express 119b; /Michael Ward 18; /Chris Ware/Keystone 49; /Stan Wayman/The LIFE Picture Collection 84b, 88t; /Robert Whitaker 14, 96-97, 101, 104, 108, 112, 113, 116, 132-133, 140-141, 148, 285; /Wolstenholme 237t

Mirrorpix: 124, 129, 131, 203, 205, 208-209

Photo12: Jean-Marie Périer 4-5

Shutterstock: 23, 47, 146, 288; /ANL 68, 81t, 156-157, 171b, 194, 270l, 271-272; /ANL/Northcliffe Collection 281; /ANL/Ronald Spencer 210; /AP 81b, 89, 118, 139, 158, 190-191, 193, 222, 268, 283; /Donald Cooper 106; /Andre Csillag 206-207; /Bob Dear 236; /Daily Mail 9; /Daily Sketch 71t, 153t, 212, 260t, 264; /Evening News 63; /Fortune/Daily Mail 147; /Tony Gibson/ANL 202b; /Sharok Hatami 43, 44, 46. 50-51, 54-55, 56, 57t; /ITV 107r, 114-115, 126; /Phillip Jackson/Daily Mail 266-267; /Peter Kemp/AP 259; /John Knoote/Daily Mail 103l; /David Magnus 52, 79, 86-87; /David McEnery 254-255; /Richard Mitchell 57b, 62; /Harry Myers 217; /New Orient 150; /Bill Orchard 134-135, 151; /Underwood Archives/UIG 280; /United Artists/Kobal 152; /Harold Valentine/AP 122, 123; /Bill Zygmant 220

Every effort has been made to acknowledge correctly and contact the source and/or copyright holder of each picture and Carlton Publishing Group apologises for any unintentional errors or omissions, which will be corrected in future editions of this book.